Double Lives, Second Chances

DOUBLE LIVES, SECOND CHANCES

The Cinema of Krzysztof Kieslowski

ANNETTE INSDORF

Foreword by Irene Jacob

tmb

**talk
miramax
books**

HYPERION

**MIRAMAX
BOOKS**

NEW YORK

791.430233092
K546
pIn7d

Library of Congress Cataloging-in-Publication Data
Insdorf, Annette.
  Double lives, second chances: the cinema of Krzysztof Kieślowski/Annette
Insdorf.—1st ed.
    p. cm.
  Filmography: p. 196
  Includes bibliographical references and index.
  ISBN 0-7868-6562-8
  1. Kieślowski, Krzysztof, 1941-   —Criticism and interpretation.
I. Title.
PN1998.3.K54I58   1999
791.43'0233'092—dc21   99-21348
                                                                      CIP

FIRST EDITION
10 9 8 7 6 5 4 3 2 1

Book design by Oksana Kushnir

FOR MARK ETHAN

CONTENTS

ACKNOWLEDGMENTS

THIS BOOK was nurtured by the seminars on Kieslowski's work that I taught at Columbia University in the Fall 1997 and Spring 1998 semesters. I am grateful to my colleagues Richard Peña and Lewis Cole for encouraging me to offer these courses, and to the students who embraced Kieslowski's bracing cinema—including Joseph Beshenkovsky, Jennifer Crean, Justine Franko, Robert Greene, Ophelia Karavias, Ji Jung-Kim, Shana Kuhn-Siegel, Sam McConnell, Melinka Thompson-Godoy, and Robert Ussery. In particular, Rahul Hamid, Marie Regan, Joanna Present, Efterpi Charambides, Amanda Davila, Noelani Riehle, Tsui-Jung Wang, and Evan Camfield made significant contributions to my understanding of Kieslowski's films.

I received tremendous assistance from Jerzy Skrzeszowski at Film Polski, who provided cassettes of Kieslowski's early work; Irena Strzalkowska and Krzysztof Zanussi at the TOR film unit; Maria Kornatowska of the Lodz Film School; and Hanka Hartowicz. For photos, Sasha Berman, Joanna Ney, Wlorzimierz Reklajtis, Stanislaw Zawislinski and especially Kristin Powers deserve thanks.

I greatly appreciate the support of Marin Karmitz—who provided necessary materials from France—as well as that of Rosine Handelman; of my agent, Georges Borchardt, and Denise Shannon.

I thank Misael Sanchez at Columbia for enabling me to view all the films with ease, and Susan Dalsimer at Miramax Books, who has been a wonderful editor. Finally, I express deepest gratitude to Dr. Cecile Insdorf—trusty translator of Polish, tireless editor of drafts, and inspirational mother.

Aᴏʀᴛᴇʀ ᴛʜᴇ critical and commercial success of his *Three Colors* trilogy—*Blue, White,* and *Red*—Krzysztof Kieslowski became one of the most internationally celebrated filmmakers in the world. Movie-lovers embraced not only his gorgeous images and compelling characters but also the deeper levels of his films: with a blend of irony and tenderness, he raises questions about behaving morally in a debased world.

No contemporary filmmaker has been more successful than Kieslowski in combining an accessible story with haunting images that suggest something beyond what we can see. His protagonists, as in *The Double Life of Veronique,* inspire viewers to wonder about spiritual existence.

This book treats Kieslowski as a cinematic poet, a Polish writer-director whose rich audio-visual vocabulary expresses a profound vision of human fallibility as well as transcendence. His motion pictures—notably *The Decalogue*—merit close analysis, especially for the ethics within their aesthetics. While examining his films' thematic, stylistic, and moral coherence, *Double Lives, Second Chances: The Cinema of Krzysztof Kieslowski* provides a detailed overview of his entire career.

The book is structured chronologically, moving from the 1960s through the 1990s. Since Kieslowski's work is not yet widely known in the United States, Chapter 1 is descriptive as well as analytical in discussing the shorts and documentaries. This first chapter includes biographical material and studies Kieslowski's early nonfiction films: these laid the groundwork for the inquisitive camera that "narrates" his later cinema.

A graduate of the famed Lodz Film School, Kieslowski began his career as an acclaimed documentary filmmaker. In recording the mundane experiences of ordinary Poles, he developed a compassionately focused gaze: "The school taught me to look at the world," he says in *Kieslowski on Kieslowski*. "It showed me that life exists, in which people talk, rejoice, worry, suffer, steal. And one could photograph all this. Then from these photographs, one could tell a story."

The focus of Chapter 2 is Kieslowski's early work in fiction, from the dramas he directed for Polish television—such as *Personnel* (1975) and *The Calm* (1976)—to his breakthrough feature, *Camera Buff* (1979).

Chapter 3 explores the dark emotional terrain of *Blind Chance* (1981)—possibly influenced by the cinema of Wojciech Has—and *No End* (1984), with special attention to the interweaving of chance and death. The section on the latter establishes the importance of such collaborators as co-writer Krzysztof Piesiewicz and composer Zbigniew Preisner.

Chapter 4 is devoted to *The Decalogue,* ten one-hour films made for Polish TV. Particular attention is paid to the two segments expanded into theatrically released features, *A Short Film about Killing* and *A Short Film about Love.*

Chapters 5 through 8 examine the international co-productions that constituted Kieslowski's last films—*The Double Life of Veronique* (1991) and the *Three Colors* trilogy—including how *Blue, White,* and *Red* were made (in France, Poland, and Switzerland). These films offer a formidable challenge to film scholars, inviting us to intimate meaning via close analysis, to discern in the concreteness of details a metaphysical weight (as in the color blue weaving through the story of a woman whose husband and child are killed in a car accident).

While incorporating research—especially in publications from France, where his work is best known and admired—*Double Lives, Second Chances: The Cinema of Krzysztof Kieslowski* is meant to be sympathetic scholarship: it should lead the reader to return to this director's motion pictures with renewed appreciation and deeper understanding.

"The world is not only bright lights, this hectic pace, the Coca-Cola with a straw, the new car. . . . Another truth exists . . . a hereafter? Yes, surely. Good or bad, I don't know, but . . . something else."

—Krzysztof Kieslowski in an interview with *Télérama*

Upon completing the reading of each script handed to me by Krzysztof, I would always find myself puzzling over certain enigmas like, Why does she touch this tree? What does she find in this shoe-lace? Why does she look at the landscape through the refracted light of her "balle magique"? (In *The Double Life of Veronique*, the character plays with a toy, a small plastic transparent sphere which can bounce, but also diffuse light in the most surprising ways.)

Then on the set, when I would ask Krzysztof what was his idea about the scene, he would usually answer, "I'd rather hear it from you, it will be more interesting for me." And if I was about to try a long explanation, he would stop me: "Oh, Irenko, that's far too complicated. Say something simpler, eh?"

He preferred not to explain his ideas of a scene on the set, but to keep a constant process of discovery open—not already codified, framed, but fresh for interpretation.

As in good literature, Krzysztof Kieslowski's films are open, to be read on many levels—but only if we can use our inner "balle magique," and receive them through the refracted light of our interpretation and re-interpretation. A few years later, I still enjoy wondering, "why does she touch the tree?" . . . and simply leave it open.

Annette Insdorf, in this wonderful study, offers an insightful reflection on Krzysztof Kieslowski's entire cinema, widening the possibilities of interpretation of each work. I revisited his films and his interviews with a new curiosity, discovering some fantastic trees I wasn't aware of—that Annette leads us to gently touch.

—Irene Jacob

CHAPTER ONE

Personal Background, Student Shorts, Documentaries

When Krzysztof Kieslowski died on March 13, 1996, at the age of fifty-four, those who knew the director and his films experienced shock, grief, and then a particularly Kieslowskian questioning. Although many of his friends had tried to dissuade him from remaining in Poland for needed bypass surgery (given a previous heart attack), he refused offers from Paris and New York—as well as two specialized open-heart-surgery centers in Poland—insisting that he was an ordinary Pole with confidence in his doctors. He walked to the Warsaw hospital, checked himself in, had the operation, and never woke up. According to his friends, the hospital was to blame, as the doctors were not sufficiently familiar with the new equipment that had been imported.[1]

Many New Yorkers learned of his death at Manhattan's Lincoln Center, where the Walter Reade Theater happened to be presenting Kieslowski's *Decalogue* throughout the week: in a rather chilling introduction, viewers settling into their seats were told that the director had just passed away. Surprised and pained, we later tried to rationalize, "Well, it's not as if we've been deprived of the films he would have made: Kieslowski announced his retirement from moviemaking after *Red*." And

John Berry, Kieslowski, Annette Insdorf, and Maurizio Nichetti.

Kieslowski at the Telluride Film Festival, 1991 Directors' Panel.

then we speculated—as do his movies—about the order of events. Did he stop making films because he knew he would die soon? Or did he believe that he had already said all he had to say and therefore felt less motivated to live? Was it by chance or destiny that he died in that hospital; or—given his refusal to go to more sophisticated medical institutions—did free will play the determining part in this drama? For a man who made the documentary *Hospital* twenty years earlier—in which Polish doctors find that instruments, electricity, and much-needed sleep are in ludicrously short supply—Warsaw was hardly the most promising place for surgery.[2]

Watching his films again, some of us were struck by the presence of death, or at least the intimations of mortality from *Blind Chance* and *No End* through *The Decalogue* and *Three Colors*. The writer Eva Hoffman recalled that when she saw Kieslowski four weeks before his death, "he wanted to live, and said his heart attack had been a warning, like that of the Polish heroine in *The Double Life of Veronique*."[3] And we listened more carefully to his seemingly offhanded remarks during television interviews. In *I'm So-So,* the 1995 documentary made for Danish television by Krsysztof Wierzbicki, he admits to being a pessimist who fears the future and sees it as a black hole. He refers to himself as a "retired film director," acknowledging that he still writes screenplays: "Someday, perhaps, a film will be made based on my writings. I hope that, in some devious way, I have laid a trap for myself so that I can stay in it forever," says the chain-smoker between coughs. When asked during a French TV interview of 1994 whether a man of fifty-three can really spend the next twenty to thirty years doing nothing, he replies, "Thirty years? I hope a person doesn't have to live that long."

The darkly ironic tone of these utterances is in keeping with Kieslowski's character. Long life was not in his genetic makeup: his father died of tuberculosis at the age of forty-seven, and his mother was killed in a car accident when she was sixty-seven. He shunned sentimentality and pretension, preferring to cast a dry eye on human folly. As an artist, he was sufficiently humble and modest to believe the world would continue quite well even if he made no new films. "I'm afraid of repeating myself," he told Wierzbicki.

I first met Kieslowski in 1980 when the New York Film Festival presented his *Camera Buff*. Although I had often translated for French directors, this was my first time as the English mouthpiece for a Polish filmmaker. But things went smoothly, and I

Annette Insdorf and Kieslowski.

Producer Richard Temtchine, Irene Jacob, and Kieslowski at the 1991
Telluride Film Festival.

ended up translating for Kieslowski throughout the 1980s and early 1990s at film festivals from Cannes to Telluride. Piercingly intelligent, he was far from demonstrative, never raising his voice—whether in a shout or a laugh. But once we got to know each other well, surprising warmth and generosity emanated from this timid, self-proclaimed pessimist. By the late 1980s, he had me calling him "Wujek" (VOO-yek, the Polish word for uncle), while his affectionate name for me was "Mala"(MA-wa, little one). He became a friend, even convincing my mother to return to Poland for the first time since the end of World War II. "You owe it to your daughter," he told her one night during the 1988 New York Film Festival. "I will pick you up at Warsaw airport and drive you to Kraków so you can show her your native city." True to his word, as he always was, one night seven months later Kieslowski drove us the five hours from Warsaw's airport to Kraków. Without his gentle insistence, my mother— who lost her family, possessions, and basic identity during the Holocaust—would never have made this extraordinary journey of return with me.

It was during this trip to Poland that I got to meet some of the most important people in Kieslowski's life, notably his wife Marysia and daughter Marta. Spending time with his corpulent composer Zbigniew Preisner, I could appreciate the counterpoint between his delicate melodies and rowdy personality. And I was able to watch cinematographer Slawomir Idziak at work, shooting Krzysztof Zanussi's *Napoleon* inside the Warsaw castle. It was in Poland that Kieslowski took my mother and me to a tiny screening room so that we could be among the first to see his magnificent *Short Film about Love*.

Perhaps because I had been François Truffaut's translator after writing a book about his cinema, I sensed similarities between the two men—especially after reading that Kieslowski watched *Citizen Kane* one hundred times, topping even Truffaut's record! As children, both watched films illictly: Truffaut played hooky to sneak into movies; Kieslowski, too poor to buy a ticket, climbed up to a roof and watched part of the screen from a vent. Both were shy autodidacts, voracious readers who wrote and directed the kind of literate films that need to be seen more than once. They made intimate motion pictures about fallible human beings for thoughtful spectators, constantly referring in interviews to their faith in the viewer. Anti-authoritarian, each had problems with military service (Kieslowski wangled his way out of the army). If Truffaut was a prolific letter-writer whose voluminous correspondence was published after his death, Kieslowski too said that for the really important things in life, he wrote letters to his daughter Marta. Devoted to their daughters, both men made films about compelling women—as well as the awkward men enamored of them.

When Truffaut died prematurely at the age of fifty-two, and Kieslowski at fifty-four, their final films each starred Jean-Louis Trintignant as a kind of stand-in for the director. In *Confidentially Yours,* he plays a timid murder suspect who falls in love with Truffaut's own romantic partner Fanny Ardant; in *Red,* Trintignant incarnates the crusty, disillusioned, retired judge who spies on his neighbors until Irene Jacob gives him a chance for warm human connection. During an interview in the French magazine *Télérama*—a special issue entitled "La Passion Kieslowski," devoted to *Three Colors*—the actor called attention to Kieslowski's tempo: "He wants me to go fast, even faster . . . like Truffaut, who also liked to make words run!"[4]

The accelerated pace at which they made their last films—at least one movie per year—leads us to ask whether they sensed they would die and therefore rushed. Or did the punishing work rhythm contribute to their early demise? When I saw Kieslowski in Paris in 1993, he looked haggard. Ordering his beloved steak tartare in La Coupole, he explained that he was editing *Blue,* shooting *White,* and refining the script for *Red.* "You're killing yourself," my mother warned him. A weary lift of the shoulders and wave of his cigarette was the only response.

Born June 27, 1941, in Warsaw, Kieslowski was constantly moving as a child. His tubercular father was a civil engineer who needed medical attention; this led the family—including his sister and his mother, an office worker—to travel around Poland. As he told journalist Joan Dupont, "My whole family was sick. I had pneumonia when I was little, my father had TB and we moved about for his cures. By the time I was 14, we had moved 40 times, traveling on trucks and trains—very good for awakening the curiosity."[5] (Perhaps because of this peripatetic existence, Kieslowski said that for his last years he wanted only the tranquillity of smoking and reading in his country home of Koczek in the Mazurian Lakes region.) He tried attending a firemen's training college but, thanks to his rebellious nature, lasted only three months. Because his family was poor, he needed a school that would provide a scholarship as well as lodging. "By chance, a relative directed a school for theater technicians in Warsaw," he explained during the 1994 New York Film Festival press conference for *Red,* as well as in a French television interview broadcast on La Sept/ARTE. "If this distant uncle had been in charge of a bank, I'd be a banker now," he added wryly.

He entered the Panstwowe Liceum Techniki Teatralnej with the intention of becoming a theater director. Because advanced studies were required, Kieslowski applied to film school as an intermediate step. He did not pass the entrance exam and was therefore a dresser at the Teatr Wspolczesny (Contemporary Theater) for a year. (Among the actors whose costumes he handled were Aleksander Bardini, Zbigniew Zapasiewicz, and Tadeusz Lomnicki, all of whom would appear in his *Decalogue* twenty years later!) Rejected a second time by the prestigious Lodz Film School—where such directors as Andrzej Wajda and Roman Polanski had studied—he spent another year as a functionary. By the third attempt, as he put it, he fiercely wanted to get in only because they had rejected him. Whether it was destiny or determination, Kieslowski was accepted.

Although he was inspired by the cinema of Fellini and Bergman, he acknowledged Ken Loach's *Kes* as the first film to truly affect him. (Years later, Kieslowski and Loach would be mutually respectful rivals for prizes at various European film festivals.) He learned from Fellini's surreal poetry, Bergman's probing rigor, and Loach's compassionate simplicity. Perhaps more centrally, he was exposed to the morally vigorous work of Krzysztof Zanussi, who was a professor at the Lodz School during Kieslowski's initial year. Zanussi, who would show up as a character in Kieslowski's *Camera Buff,* had already made the prize-winning short, *Death of a Provincial* (1965): as many of Kieslowski's films would do, it reflects on themes like faith and death. (On a personal note, it was during Kieslowski's final year of studies that he married his wife Marysia.)

The rise of postwar Polish cinema would be unimaginable without the Lodz Film School, created in 1948. For a nation whose geographical and political existence has been truncated for centuries, art becomes a means to sustain national identity. And, as Lenin put it, film is "the most important art" in twentieth-century Europe. Once known for its textile factories, Lodz attracted the best and the brightest. As Slawomir Idziak—who was a cinematography student at the same time Kieslowski was training to be a director—told me in November of 1998:

Film school in Lodz was absolutely unique. During Communism, it was an island of free spirit . . . the place to see movies normally censored for the public in Poland. It was the place where all the internationally recognized artists visiting Poland were invited. And, most important, we had the best Polish directors and cameramen as teachers. Poland was a secluded country, and for all these people cut off from the outside world, film school was the place to see each other and discuss openly topics that were not very welcome in my country.

When New York's Museum of Modern Art celebrated the fiftieth anniversary of the Lodz Film School with a retrospective in December 1998, Joshua Siegel—assistant curator of the Department of Film and Video—wrote a richly contextualizing and comprehensive essay. "From 1772 to 1795, the Polish

Commonwealth . . . was carved up by Russia, Germany and Austria," he explains in the brochure. "For the next 123 years, Poland vanished from the map of Europe, as the three mighty empires waged battle with one another." But even after Germany and Austria signed the Treaty of Versailles in 1919, recognizing Poland as an independent nation, hostile neighbors and economic devastation prevented the country from developing. By 1939, Hitler's Germany and Stalin's Russia forged their Non-aggression Pact to carve up Poland and the Baltic States. Nazi occupation was followed by Soviet occupation.

After World War II, the political climate in Poland was extremely tense. As Stalin once acknowledged, introducing Communism in Poland was like fitting a cow with a saddle. While many Poles embraced Communism, having fought the Nazis alongside the Red Army, others fiercely rejected it. Indeed, much of the Polish resistance during World War II had been in the AK (Armia Krajowa), the Polish Home Army, which was as anti-Communist (and anti-Semitic) as it was anti-Nazi. Siegel, citing Norman Davies's seminal book *Heart of Europe: A Short History of Poland,* adds:

> Poland became a Stalinist one-party State. By 1946 the State had taken away over ninety percent of Poland's industrial production, and sweeping land reforms broke up the prewar Polish estates. Heavy industry was given precedence over agricultural production, and the general standard of living declined as the private sector was abolished and workers were exploited. . . . Anyone suspected of disloyalty was interrogated, censored, or put in prison. Though the terrorist practices were rarely as grave as those inflicted on Hungary or Czechoslovakia, and the farms were never collectivized, Stalinism in Poland was a combination of brutality and compromise.

Although the Lodz School was founded under the auspices of the newly created Film Polski—a state-run organization funded by the Ministry of Culture and Art—and was originally designed to encourage Stalinist propaganda, it took on a free life of its own. The school flourished in spite of a repressive political system, especially under Stalin, but also thanks to censorship: irony, circumvention, and metaphor are sharp tools when ideas can't be expressed directly. After Stalin's death in 1953, under the leadership of Jerzy Toeplitz, the Lodz School abandoned Socialist Realism for social realism. And its graduates were aided by a new state system of *zespoly*, semi-autonomous units allowing a measure of creative freedom. Although still subject to government censorship—requiring submission of the script and later of the finished movie—filmmakers benefited from a buffer: many of the units were headed by filmmakers of the stature of Andrzej Wajda (*X*) and Zanussi (*Tor*), in a system that continues to the present day.

During a comprehensive colloquium devoted to Kieslowski's work at the Paris Vidéothèque on June 17, 1997, the French critic Michel Ciment proposed a succinct overview of periods in Polish cinema. If the first wave in the 1950s included directors like Wajda, Jerzy Kawalerowicz, Wojciech Has, and Andrzej Munk—in a "dialogue with history" not without romanticism —followed by the second wave in the early 1960s with Polanski and Jerzy Skolimowski, the third wave consisted of Zanussi and Kieslowski in "a return to the quotidian and the pessimistic."

Kieslowski's first two student shorts in 1966—both approximately 6 minutes, shot in 35mm black and white—indicate the dual directions in which his cinema would develop. *The Office* (*Urzad*) is a satiric documentary about bureaucracy. In a state-run insurance office, impersonality is heightened by the fact that—despite a lot of dialogue—we rarely see people's lips moving. The emphasis is on what kind of rubber stamps are needed on forms. A clerk says the office has nothing to do with an elderly woman's request. Files sit on shelves, tea is made, and we hear the repetition of a female voice instructing someone, "Write down what you did to support yourself all your life."

The Tram (*Tramwaj*), on the other hand, is a fictional short that introduces the Kieslowskian intertwining of romance and voyeurism. A young man catches a bus and then stares at an attractive young woman. She smiles at him after he closes the door that was causing a draft, and then she falls asleep. He gets off at his stop, continues to gaze at the receding vehicle with the sleeping beauty, and suddenly runs after the bus. In his frustration, the young man can be seen as an embryonic version of the awkward voyeur Tomek in *A Short Film about Love*.

The professor credited as supervisor on *The Tram* was Wanda Jakubowska. Twenty years earlier, she had directed the first fiction feature about—and shot in—Auschwitz, where she had been a political prisoner: *The Last Stop* (also known as *The Last Stage*) is a powerful black-and-white drama about female solidarity in the concentration camp. Jakubowska then oversaw Kieslowski's *Concert of Wishes* (*Koncert Zyczen*, 1967), a 17-minute fiction short that once again portrays an outsider to romance. As rock music plays from a bus radio in the background, a group of young men drink and fool around by a lake. A bespectacled youth spies a couple in the bushes, and stares at the girl. The couple leaves on a motorcycle, followed by the bus. When the motorcycle passes the bus, their bag (containing an inflatable tent) falls off. The vulgar louts in the bus won't give it back unless she travels with them—which she seems tempted to do—but they finally let her go with her boyfriend. The bespectacled young man looks after her wistfully as they recede from view.

Kieslowski's early work, while engaging, hardly suggests the brilliance that would develop later in his career. He gradually grew into an artist by learning his craft, observing the world closely, and later developing a personal vision. His subsequent shorts were primarily documentaries, and his written thesis in 1968 for the Lodz Film School ennobled nonfiction filmmaking: "A reality that is rich, magnificent, incommensurable,

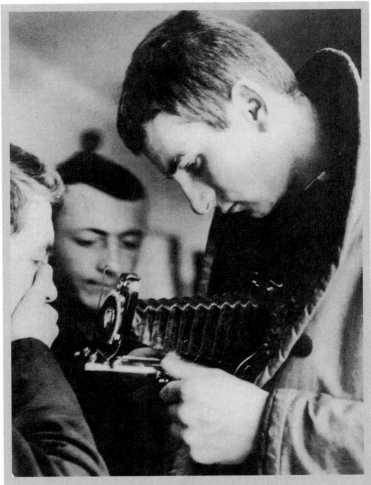

Kieslowski as a young man, from the Polish photo album *O Kieslowskim*.

where nothing is repeated, where one cannot redo a take. We don't have to worry about its development: it will continue to provide us daily with new and extraordinary shots. Reality—and this is not a paradox—is the point of departure for the document. One merely has to believe totally in the dramaturgy of reality."[6] He cites people committed to recording life's complexity—from critic André Bazin to directors Robert Flaherty and Richard Leacock—and celebrates editing as a creative process.

Among the professors in Lodz was Kazimierz Karabacz, who had directed a 10-minute documentary in 1958 entitled *Sunday Musicians*. This short must have made quite an impression on Kieslowski: when he was asked in 1994 to list the ten greatest films, *Sunday Musicians* was the only unknown title. (Kieslowski's other choices—in no particular order—were Fellini's *La Strada*, Ken Loach's *Kes*, Bresson's *A Man Escaped*, Bo Widerberg's *The Pram*, Ivan Passer's *Intimate Lighting*, Tarkovsky's *Ivan's Childhood*, Truffaut's *The 400 Blows*, Welles's *Citizen Kane*, and Chaplin's *The Kid*. However, his list for *Sight and Sound* has Tony Richardson's *Loneliness of the Long Distance Runner* in place of *The 400 Blows*.)

Sunday Musicians records how two dozen older male workers play their instruments under the leadership of an aging conductor. After making awkward sounds, they finally arrive at recognizable music. "It is rare for a short to express so many things, in a manner so beautiful and simple, about the need to create which is inherent in human beings," wrote Kieslowski in 1994. "Because, in addition to satisfying our elementary needs—survival, eating breakfast, lunch, dinner, and sleeping after work— we all aspire to something which gives meaning to our life and elevates it."[7]

Kieslowski's early work developed in this direction, addressing ordinary lives in all their poetry and poignancy. This approach began with *The Photo* (*Zdjecie*, 1968), in which he searches for two now-grown men who posed for a photograph when they were little boys. If, as Ralph Waldo Emerson put it, "the invariable mark of wisdom is to find the miraculous in the common," Kieslowski became an especially wise filmmaker. Painfully aware of the discrepancy between screen images and the daily life of most Polish people, he turned his quietly inquisitive camera to a real—if bleak—world.

Politics hovered in the background. As Joshua Siegel points out in the Museum of Modern Art program notes:

> Gomulka was being pressured by nationalistic, anti-Semitic, anti-intellectual forces within the Communist Party. As head of the security police and the Interior Ministry, General Mieczyslaw Moczar had substantial military muscle. Moczar and his propagandists claimed that the Jews were part of an imperialist Soviet (or sometimes West German) conspiracy to overthrow Poland, pointing to the second Arab–Israeli war (which began in 1967), the Czech Spring of 1968, and the student demonstrations that were breaking out at universities across Poland as evidence of a Zionist Fifth Column. In fact, the government was engineering student demonstrations to set the media and the workers against the intellectuals. Like many protesters, Krzysztof Kieslowski did not realize this until after the damage had been done.

The director admitted to interviewers:

> [T]he more I shouted against the authorities, the more I threw those stones, the more people would get thrown out of the country. . . . We were used. I realized I could never have anything to do with politics because politics deceived the students. It was a very important period for me and my generation. Some of my friends and their parents were exiled and it was a horrifying experience to see their empty apartments. We helped them with their luggage and saw them off every day at the railway station to Vienna. We would sing a farewell: Peace! Peace! You will rot in the ports, Bolsheviks, and I will still have relations with the Jewish people.[8]

Anti-Semitic and anti-intellectual purges took place not only in universities and scientific centers but in the cultural community as well. Toeplitz was forced to resign as rector of the Lodz

School (he became the head of the new Australian Film, Television and Radio School); Aleksander Ford—Toeplitz's predecessor and founder of the First Polish Army's Film Unit during World War II—was expelled from the Party and forced into exile; and two-thirds of Poland's remaining Jews were compelled to emigrate. As Slawomir Idziak explained to me, "Everybody in Poland knew that the film school was a paradise but, for sure, not a Communist paradise. This is probably why in 1968 the film school was the first place to be attacked by Communist anti-Semitic propaganda as a reactionary nest. The School lost a lot of professors and students." Kieslowski's pessimism was probably nurtured by the purges of 1968, as well as the futile strikes that followed in 1970 in response to food shortages and government-imposed price increases. This was the time in which Gomulka was replaced by Edward Gierek, who would lead Poland until the rise of the Solidarity movement in 1980. As Kieslowski told an interviewer, "To be a Pole . . . means that each generation has had a hope which was deceived at the end, which didn't materialize. And to know that from the very beginning, that it will end like this. We will have the hope and then we will be beaten anyway." [9]

From the City of Lodz (*Z Miasta Lodzi*, 1969), Kieslowski's graduating film, was also his first professional endeavor, co-produced by the Lodz Film School and the WFD (State Documentary Film Studios in Warsaw). What had been a glorious industrial center in the nineteenth century is presented as a gray mass of ruins, its citizens lacking vitality. In *I'm So-So,* Kieslowski piercingly describes Lodz in terms of "people's sad faces with a dramatic meaninglessness in their eyes." He shows everything but productive work: in a factory, women do an exercise drill to loosen their arms; in the street, men seem to wander aimlessly; workers complain about a lack of support for their orchestra; a woman who is retiring says she would like to continue working but cannot; in the park, amateur singers croon a few songs. As Kieslowski elaborated in *I'm So-So,* he felt the need to show a reality that was not visible on-screen:

Z Miasta Lodzi

"Our descriptive tools had been used for propagandistic purposes. . . . Outside Poland, you don't know what it means to live in a world without representation."

I Was a Soldier (Bylem Zolnierzem, 1970) is one of Kieslowski's most powerful documentaries, not only for its moving subject matter—men blinded during military service in World War II—but also for its understated treatment. We do not know at the outset of the black-and-white film what links these men, each speaking in close-up. There are hints: some wear dark glasses; others speak of seeing in the past tense only. A printed title on a white screen—"I ask the doctors, 'what time is it?' "—is followed by their quiet voicing of despair: one asks, "Now I'm blind—why live?" while another says, "I prefer to vanish from the earth." A second white-out to a title introduces a section about the soldiers' vividly visual dreams: as one veteran puts it, "In dreams I see everything." The third title, "The war is to blame," precedes their expression of anti-war feelings and hope for peace.

Each white-out to a title is accompanied by classical harpsichord music, an appropriate musical expression of Kieslowski's narrative strategy. The contrapuntal music is analogous to the montage of different faces and voices contributing to the whole. *I Was a Soldier* also contains a gentle self-consciousness: the men seem to be sitting around a table, and there is just enough visual obstruction—a leaf? a branch?—to make us aware that even we can't see everything clearly. Eschewing long shots or even master shots, the film permits no easy overview. (There are curious symmetries in Kieslowski's oeuvre: if, eight years later, he would make *Seven Women of Different Ages* about females in the world of dance, *I Was a Soldier* presents seven men of different ages in the context of war.)

Factory (*Fabryka*, 1970) and *Before the Rally* (*Przed Rajdem*, 1971) depict Poland's economic limitations, whether those of a tractor factory lacking equipment due to bureaucracy, or of two Polish drivers preparing for the Monte Carlo rally: because their Polish Fiat is under-par, they can't even complete the race. The former is again structured by montage, as Kieslowski crosscuts between physical labor in the Ursus tractor factory and the belabored verbalizing of a management board meeting. The latter is notable for the counterpoint between image and harpsichord music—a classical contrast to chaotic events.

Refrain (*Refren*, 1972) refines the darkly humorous tone already found in *The Office*, Kieslowski's first short: in a funeral parlor, bureaucracy reigns. A bereaved client is told that if a man died on a certain street, he has to be buried in a different cemetery than the one requested. Another client is lectured that you can get a grave only with a death certificate. The last—and quintessentially Kieslowskian—shot is of numbers being put on newborn babies. If death is a methodical business, the ending wryly suggests that bureaucracy begins at birth. *Refrain* is thus in keeping with a 1971 filmmakers' manifesto—signed by Kieslowski—that called for documentary films to be more aggressive in confronting bureaucracy, corruption, and cant.

Refrain

A far more optimistic tone can be found in the two documentaries commissioned by the Lubin copper mine, *Between Wroclaw and Zielona Gora* (*Miedzy Wroclawlem a Zielona Gora*, 1972) and *The Principles of Safety and Hygiene in a Copper Mine* (*Podstawy BHP w Kopalni Miedzi*, 1972). The first is narrated by a young male worker who arrived seven months earlier in this new city located between Wroclaw and Zielona Gora. He praises not only his working conditions but Lubin itself, where he helps to make apartment houses that are "sprouting like mushrooms after rain." Images of new living complexes, schools, shops, theaters, and sports areas support his description of "a city bursting with life, waking up." *The Principles of Safety*—Kieslowski's only documentary with an omniscient third-person narrator—is a training film. With a focus on the same worker as in *Between Wroclaw and Zielona Gora*, we learn what to do in a mine. The most entertaining part is what not to do—like jumping out of an underground train—often shown via cartoon drawings of the consequences.

Workers '71

Workers '71 (*Robotnicy '71,* 1972) returns to the more personal and somber tonality of Kieslowski's observations. Co-directed with Tomasz Zygadlo, this 46-minute documentary is subtitled *Nothing about Us without Us* (*Nic o nas bez nas*) and takes the temperature of Poland after the December 1970 strikes. Like a fly on the proverbial wall, the camera takes in varieties of frustration, from workers' complaints in a factory, to a widow asking for the factory's orchestra to play at her husband's funeral, to men voting for delegates to the Communist Party congress. As in *Before the Rally,* the classical music—played on guitar—feels contrapuntal, suggesting an ordered universe far from these confused citizens.

During the 1997 Paris colloquium, Kieslowski's colleague Marcel Lozinski—himself a leading documentary filmmaker—recalled the climate in which they made their films:

> During the early 1970s, we felt a little hope with Gierek's arrival, after the anti-Semitic and anti-intellectual events of

1968. There had been total liberty at the film school, although the best—mostly Jewish—professors had to leave. The situation was paradoxical: almost all the films we shot were shelved. But Kieslowski cleverly explained to the Vice Minister of Culture that if they made 90% propaganda films, a few per year from the other side [of the political spectrum, or the opposition] could be useful to him for the future—if a new group were in power. This worked.

Bricklayer (*Murarz,* 1973) juxtaposes the public and the private, the official celebration of May Day with the intimate voice-over of a man acknowledging doubt and disappointment. The film's dual focus is embodied by a tracking shot of forty-five-year-old Jozef Malesa through a bus window: he coexists with the reflection of Warsaw's streets. While he and his friends prepare to march in the procession, his narration provides a

Bricklayer

capsule summary of his life—from youthful enthusiasm ("We all thought we were making a revolution"), to his ascent into bureaucratic power, to disillusionment in 1956, culminating in a return to masonry. The parade extols masses with slogans, but Kieslowski's film focuses on one quiet voice. It ends with an aerial shot of Warsaw's streets as Malesa's voice expresses pride in his work. The rows of brick houses seem to support the mason's concluding statement: the solidity of what he built gives him the sense that he didn't waste his life.

With *The Railway Station* (*Dworzec,* 1980), Kieslowski creates a more pointed juxtaposition of official optimism and private frustration. Shot over ten nights at Warsaw's Central Station, it begins with a television news announcer talking about production figures on the rise. This bears little relation to the sad faces of people waiting in the station. His voice yields, appropriately, to that of a woman announcing a delayed train—Polish reality indeed. "Why are so many trains canceled?" asks a man. "Fewer passengers, they say," is the answer, leaving the skeptical viewer to suspect it is the other way round. When a delayed train finally arrives, people run to catch it; others must remain, waiting with stony faces in the cheerless station.

This would have been enough to render *The Railway Station* a strikingly authentic document of real life in Poland. But after shooting most of the film, Kieslowski went a step further by punctuating it with shots of a surveillance camera in the station. The first five times that we see the camera swivel, timpani drums on the soundtrack create an ominous feeling. By the seventh and eighth appearances of the camera, there are no drums, as Kieslowski crosscuts between the surveillance machinery and people in the station watching a TV screen (a female announcer has prepared them for "an English film, *My Friend Spot"*). *The Railway Station* ends with the man behind the camera: remote, impassive, pressing buttons for the multiple screens, he keeps his eye on the station. Unlike the TV announcer at the beginning,

Railway Station

he is invisible; nevertheless, he is just as detached from the waiting passengers.

A profoundly more hopeless kind of waiting informs *X-Ray* (*Przeswietlenie,* 1974), set in a tuberculosis sanatorium. Four men acknowledge their feelings of sadness, uselessness, and self-doubt. Reminiscent of *I Was a Soldier,* each is seen in close-up, lamenting his inability to live fully and productively while protected in the sanatorium. Although Kieslowski might have been drawn to the subject because of his own father's fatal illness, *X-Ray* introduces a theme that would be developed in his *Three Colors* trilogy—the plight of the individual who isolates himself from the world.

As he told a French interviewer in 1979, "When I make a fiction film, I always know how it will end. When I shoot a documentary, I don't. And it's exciting to not know how the shot will end, not to mention the whole film. For me, the documentary is a greater art form than fiction filmmaking because I think life is more intelligent than I am. It creates more interesting situations than I could invent on my own."[10] This was certainly the case with *First Love* (*Pierwsza Milosc,* 1974), which marked a turning point in Kieslowski's career.

Despite the title, *First Love* is hardly a romantic film. Instead of presenting images of desire, courtship, or erotic contact, it documents how a pregnant seventeen-year-old and her boyfriend officially become a couple. We meet Jadwiga in the office of a doctor who warns her that an abortion would be too dangerous. Roman is introduced during a medical exam for military service. If we were expecting kisses and dates, Kieslowski shifts us to the reality of bureaucracy and compromise.

At the housing office where they hope to speed up the assignment of an apartment, a woman tells them it's still a three-year wait. They must live in a spare room at Jadwiga's grandmother's apartment. While they are painting the cramped space, a policeman arrives: they are not registered at this address and, he adds wryly, this former kitchen is too small for the three of them to call home. (Kieslowski admitted to some creative tampering by being the one, "with clear provocation," who sent in the policeman: "I deliberately found a policeman whom I thought wouldn't cause much harm, although Jadzia was in her eighth month by then and the whole thing could have been quite risky—an unexpected visit like that could have induced labour."[11])

Their wedding is far from glamorized: we see that they have to pay a fee for the civil service, where background noise competes with the ceremony. Jadwiga's mother and then her father tell the tearful bride that they hope her marriage will be happier than theirs. Kieslowski replaces Hollywood (or European screen) romance with the overwhelming realities young lovers face in Poland. For example, a young mother casually asks Jadwiga in the park if she isn't afraid her baby might be born handicapped. And when she goes to her high school for the report card, Jadwiga confronts the condescension of teachers: as a female instructor puts it, her grade of C for behavior reflects not only Jadwiga's absences but her bad example as a pregnant seventeen-year-old.

Kieslowski's unintrusive yet revelatory camera documents the birth, including Jadwiga's visible pain, insufficient oxygen pumps, a nurse complaining how understaffed they are, and buzzers ringing in the background. When Roman is told of his baby girl, he tearfully calls his mother. The film ends with the couple beside the baby's crib, talking about their hopes for her in the future—to be wiser than them, and to be as happy as they are now.

It's not surprising that *First Love* temporarily led Kieslowski away from documentaries, as he felt morally discomfitted by intruding on the couple's intimacy. "The documentary camera doesn't have the right to enter what interests me most," he said on French television, "the intimate, private life of individuals. I preferred to buy glycerine at the pharmacy, and actors to simulate crying, than to film real people crying, or making love, or dying." This essentially moral stance led him to make fiction dramas for television, beginning in 1975 with *Personnel*. Nevertheless, Kieslowski's filmography in the late 1970s is punctuated by nonfiction shorts in between narrative features. Having directed thirty documentaries, he could declare, "Documentary filmmaking is a very good school for synthetic thinking in the cinema."[12]

In 1976, he spent almost five months shooting *Hospital (Szpital)*, an unsettling 35-minute portrait of orthopedic surgeons working a 32-hour shift in a Warsaw hospital. Without commentary, he simply presents the hospital as a workplace: doctors are workers who—as he put it many years later—"want to help, but lack the means." They smoke, try (unsuccessfully) to eat, and are paid. But because of his rigorously chronological structure—titles specify each hour's passage—a grimly comic tone pervades: overworked doctors do their best despite intermittent electricity, shoddy instruments, and a mere two-hour nap amid a flurry of nonstop operations. On French TV, the director recalled the audience response: "They understood that we were filming 'in a drop of water,' that *Hospital* represented a larger reality in which people want to improve things, but can't because the structure is deplorable."

Hospital

Kieslowski's documentaries eschew the voice-over commentary of an omniscient narrator, preferring to simply present people, places, and processes to the viewer. One of the best examples of this "objective" stance is *From a Night Porter's Point of View* (*Z Punktu Widzenia Nocnego Portiera*, 1977). The factory worker Marian Osuch is a strict disciplinarian who believes that "rules are more important than people." During the 17-minute portrait, he goes from talking about the kinds of films he likes to praising capital punishment. "I don't think he's a bad man," Kieslowski observed. "I suspect he's quite an ordinary human being. He just happens to think that it would be a good thing to hang people publicly because that would make everybody else afraid to commit crimes. . . . It comes from his not too high level of intelligence, from a rather vulgar attitude to life and the environment he was brought up in."[13] Osuch saw and liked the film, but when Polish television tried to show *From a Night Porter's Point of View*, Kieslowski objected, fearing it could cause the porter humiliation. (Despite the straightforwardness of this

From a Night Porter's Point of View

documentary, it includes music by Wojciech Kilar, the film composer best known for his collaborations with Zanussi and Wajda.)

I Don't Know (Nie Wiem, 1977) is a more extreme example of Kieslowski's reticence to publicly show a documentary that might harm his subject. For 46 minutes, an engineer who was the director of a factory in Lower Silesia for nine years tells his story matter-of-factly to the camera. He was a Party member who found that people in his factory were stealing leather. But he didn't realize that these workers were in collusion with the provincial police as well as the Party Committee. Once he opposed the Party, he was dismissed. After the film was shot, Kieslowski took two measures to protect the engineer: whenever he names someone, the brief, loud sound of a typewriter covers the name. The second measure was more drastic, as Kieslowski tried to stop the film from airing on television. He succeeded, and *I Don't Know* was never shown anywhere. Since it begins and ends in the same way—tango music and a title

I Don't Know

stating we should listen to this man talking about his life—the film suggests that nothing changes.

A cyclical structure also informs *Seven Women of Different Ages (Siedem Kobiet W Roznym Wieku,* 1978)—winner at the 1979 Kraków Film Festival—which is set in a girls' ballet school. "Thursday," the focus is on a pretty child. "Friday" offers an adolescent student in class. "Saturday" presents an older class whose central young woman resembles the younger dancers of the preceding segments. On "Sunday," we are treated to a performance of a romantic pas de deux with yet another dancer. A different duo rehearses on "Monday," as we hear the grunts of physical exertion rather than music. On "Tuesday," a middle-aged woman waits for the result of a casting announcement and learns that she will be a backup dancer. The focus of "Wednesday" is an older teacher of a very young ballet class. The seven days of the week—as well as the arc from childhood to advanced age—provide the cyclical structure. Time is passing and renewing as Kieslowski casts a sympathetic gaze at women in the dance world. (One can even see in the first little girl who poses and stretches a hint of Valentine at her dance class in *Red*.) Unlike the predominantly male subjects of his preceding documentaries, *Seven Women of Different Ages* paves the way for the compelling female figures of his final four films.

Kieslowski's canvas widens in *Talking Heads* (*Gadajace Glowy*, 1980), a fascinating interrogation on what Polish people want. In this veritable "Concert of Wishes," we hear Kieslowski's voice asking three questions: When were you born? Who are you really? What do you want most? The year of birth is printed on the screen, going from 1979—a baby is on-camera—to children born in the late 1970s, to increasingly older speakers. He interviewed 100 Poles between the ages of 7 and 100, of whom 40 remain in the film. The majority sound idealistic, compassionate, and overwhelmingly democratic. The ironic punch line is provided by the last subject: "I'd like to live longer!" is the reply of the 100-year-old woman.

Seven Women of Different Ages

In 1988, a Rotterdam production company headed by Dick Rijneke commissioned a few directors to make an international compilation film, *City Life,* set in places including Calcutta (Mrinal Sen), Buenos Aires (Alejandro Agresti), and Houston (Eagle Pennell). *Seven Days a Week (Siedem Dni W Tygodnui)* was Kieslowski's 18-minute contribution, a documentary moving around Warsaw from Monday to Saturday. On each day, we see part of a different person's life: Monday, a man washes (someone knocks before he is finished), stands on a bus, and works in a factory; Tuesday, a woman tidies up her small home—turning a bed back into a day couch—before cleaning someone else's place and preparing their meal; Wednesday, a younger man tutors a child in Russian and then works as a typist (his text is "The Politburo's Holiday Session"); Thursday, a young woman is a guide for an American orchestra in the morning and a paramedic by afternoon; Friday, a ponytailed drummer marks his own space in an apartment by placing his freshly painted sneakers on parts of the floor; Saturday, an elderly woman waits endlessly on a post office line for her pension, then on an embassy

Seven Days a Week

line for a visa, then on a butcher line for her piece of sausage. It is only when these people sit down at the same breakfast table on Sunday that we realize they are all members of one family. By the end of the week, three generations of Warsaw residents have survived a round of daily realities including cramped space, double workloads, and bureaucracy.

The best of Kieslowski's early films are about time, marking its passage by hour (*Hospital*), by day (*Seven Women of Different Ages*), by year (*Talking Heads*), and by larger cycles of death and birth (*Refrain*). In a similar vein, his collaborators have remarked upon the director's tendency to count how much celluloid he has shot and how much remains—an obsession with time as measured by film. Like the Jewish prayer that asks, "Teach us to number our days, that we may attain a heart of wisdom," Kieslowski's work reflects a profound awareness: the limitations define the possibilities.

CHAPTER TWO

Early Fiction

AFTER MAKING thirty documentaries, Kieslowski acknowledged his discomfort with the format during a 1995 interview in a Polish newspaper:

> I began with the documentary. I abandoned it because every nonfiction filmmaker ends up realizing one day the boundaries that can't be crossed—those beyond which we risk causing harm to the people we film. That's when we feel the need to make fiction features.[1]

The second stage of his career consisted of reality-based fiction films like *The Calm*. From 1973 to 1979, both Polish television and the TOR *zespol* (the state-funded Polish "unit" or production house headed by Zanussi) afforded Kieslowski the opportunity to hone his craft in terms of screenplays, staging, and directing performers. The films grew in length from *Pedestrian Subway* (30 minutes) and *Curriculum Vitae* (45 minutes), to *Personnel* (72 minutes) and *The Scar* (104 minutes). They constitute a transition, as Kieslowski's cinema evolved from what he considered a necessary description of external reality to intimations of interior (and multiple) possibilities. He expanded from black-and-white to color, and from documentary detail to poetic mise-en-scène.

The effect of his films was bracing, as Josef Tischner—a well-known Polish priest and philosopher who delivered Kieslowski's funeral oration—recalled during the 1997 Paris colloquium. After invoking Auschwitz as an indirect context for Kieslowski's work, he said, "His camera shows a destroyed world—not just the physical landscape, but the human. In terms of Polish art, this is a new form of melancholy—not despair, but a deep melancholy where every act is drained of meaning. His films were a kind of intellectual and spiritual cleansing for viewers accustomed to seeing the world through images approved by the government." Even at an early stage of his career, artists looked to Kieslowski for guidance—not merely aesthetic, but moral—and he became head of the TOR film unit in 1984.

His first major experience with professional actors was *Pedes-*

Kieslowski with editor Dorota Werduskiewicz

trian Subway (*Przejscie Podziemne,* 1973), a television drama starring Teresa Budisz-Krzyzanowska as a shop decorator and Andrzej Seweryn as her estranged husband. A teacher in a small town, the husband comes to see his wife in the hope she will return. The film depicts essentially a one-night stand between a man and woman about to be divorced. But the setting makes *Pedestrian Subway* distinctive: because of the centrality of the shop window, Kieslowski and cinematographer Slawomir Idziak (in their first of many collaborations) explore inner frames and voyeurism.

It was Kieslowski's idea to set the action in a metro underpass that had just opened in the center of Warsaw. He co-wrote the script with Ireneusz Iredynski and then shot the black-and-white film in nine nights. Dissatisfied, however, he decided on the tenth and last night to change the entire film. Using a documentary camera, he reshot all the scenes, having encouraged the actors to improvise. The result is a "subterranean" film indeed, spatially and emotionally. The wet pavement and garish neon light prefigure the last shots of *A Short Film about Killing* (also photographed by Idziak). The lack of exteriors creates a claustrophobic feeling: when the teacher first enters the store, for example, a round lamp prominent in the shot crowds him.

The voyeurism that would become a central theme in *A Short Film about Love* takes shape here: because his wife's legs are revealed as a man passes by, the teacher throws water at the window to obstruct the stranger's view. Whereas others can look in at them, once he puts newspaper on the window, the couple on the inside watch what happens in the underpass. Through the masked frame of a hole in the newspaper, for instance, the teacher sees a man being beaten up. When they finally make love on the floor next to the window, the audience's own voyeurism is frustrated because little passion is visible. *Pedestrian Subway* ends with the wife's unsentimental good-bye and the husband's exit up into a white sky.

This juxtaposition of a fictional plot and a real setting would be developed in *Curriculum Vitae* (*Zycioris,* also translated as

Biography or *Life Story,* 1975), about a Communist Party Control Committee interrogating a Party member who has been expelled. Although the screenplay was written by Kieslowski and Janusz Fastyn, the central role of Gralak was played by an engineer who had been harassed by—and thrown out of—the Party. Moreover, the Party Committee questioners are indeed Communist Party members playing themselves. Kieslowski had gone to numerous Party Committees and asked them for "the most enlightened, the most liberal, the most circumspect Party board of Control in Warsaw."[2] Even these "best" prove to be crude meddlers in the private life of the protagonist, bringing up issues like his church wedding (of which they don't approve) or an extramarital affair eight years earlier.

The docudrama begins with people sitting down to a long table where they will consider Gralak's appeal. Shots of this room are crosscut with Gralak on his way to the meeting; whereas there is no music with the (mostly male) Committee, a curiously percussive soundtrack accompanies the protagonist. "Pong" sounds (as in Jacques Rivette's *La Religieuse*) create ten-

Curriculum Vitae

sion and add the counterpoint of a cinematic self-consciousness to the documentary-like images.

During the meeting, faces in close-up are starkly lit against a black background. The authentic feel of the proceedings is intensified by formal imperfections: Gralak is occasionally blocked from the camera's view by someone moving—and smoking—in the foreground; people interrupt each other, creating a realistic babble. The interrogators are polite, but they seem to have already decided that Gralak is hotheaded: they question the way he does things more than the actions themselves. As he awaits their decision about his appeal, we see photos of a younger Gralak, ending with a snapshot of the boy in a uniform fading to a white screen. Kieslowski thus shows us what the Committee seems to ignore— the evolution of a human life. We never learn their decision.

Kieslowski wrote and directed a stage version of *Curriculum Vitae* in 1978, which ran for approximately one month at the Stary Theater in Kraków. (He also directed for television William Gibson's play, *Two for the Seesaw*.) While he considered his "C.V." stage adaptation a mistake, the experience might have provided some of the background for his next film, *Personnel* (*Personel*, also translated as *The Staff*, 1975). Set behind the scenes of a theater, it depicts the rite of passage of nineteen-year-old Romek (Juliusz Machulski, who went on to become a director of films including *Sex Mission*). Working as a tailor in the wardrobe department, the naive youth learns that his lofty ideals about art are illusory: theater is simply a business, and an unpleasantly politicized one at that.

Romek's uncertainty about who he is takes complex visual shape in the film's opening credit sequence: as props are being transported, he, and the audience, see a fleeting reflection of Romek in five consecutive mirrors that are moved past him. The emphasis throughout *Personnel* is on his gaze: Romek takes everything in on his first day, from a massive prop of a horse being lowered outside the window to a pair of dancers rehearsing a pas de deux. Later, he watches a ballet rehearsal (prefiguring Kieslowski's subsequent documentary, *Seven Women of*

Different Ages); from a very high angle, he looks in wonder at a stage rehearsal; he peers at a violinist rehearsing; and he finally attends the opening of the opera. Only in the last two scenes of *Personnel* does he wear glasses, suggesting a new way of looking more sharply at the world.

Political coming-of-age is part of Romek's apprenticeship in the wardrobe department. His colleague Sowa (Michal Tarkowski) tries a costume he has made on the soloist Andrzej. The singer is thrilled with the outfit. But after Andrzej plays a practical joke on Romek with an exploding cigarette, Sowa's displeasure sets the singer off. When the costumes are examined onstage by the opera heads, Andrzej complains that his is badly sewn. All puffed up literally and figuratively, he stretches so that the costume rips. This leads to Sowa being reprimanded at a meeting of the workers. Instead of defending himself, he argues that their problems are greater than a costume, berating the group for staging old plays to half-empty theaters. In the background, a silent man with glasses takes notes—probably the spy for Party officials.

Because Romek is vocal at the meeting—suggesting a cabaret run by the workers, for example—the head of the technicians offers Romek secret assistance with finding an apartment, and with school, if he "works with" them. What this means becomes apparent in the last scene, when Romek is summoned by the director of the opera (played by the real head of the Wroclaw Opera), who asks him to write a letter about the Sowa incident. Will the confused Romek succumb and denounce his friend? The film ends abruptly with him not writing. However, there is ambiguity when the end credits crosscut shots of Romek still sitting at the desk in the intense sunlight of the director's office: because the camera is positioned so far away, it is difficult to see whether he is writing or not.

Stylistically intriguing, *Personnel* feels like a documentary: the camera is hand-held; pieces of cloth occasionally flutter before the lens, briefly obscuring characters in the background; the wardrobe men are real tailors who are actually sewing while talking. On the other hand, at least two self-conscious shots point to Kieslowski's future style. Building on the multiple mirrors of the opening, a scene behind the stage is expressionistic: Romek's elderly guide says (voice-off) that "working in theater is like flying" as we see Romek moving down a long, narrow passageway. The chiaroscuro lighting charges the frame with drama, especially when he approaches the camera into the light. In close-up, his face seems to be rising, as if on an elevator, literalizing the idea of flying.

Romek's face in close-up is once again the focus of the drama when he attends the opening with his aunt. The light diminishes and then slowly grows full on his expectant face as the overture begins. The angle tells us what is important in this scene—not the opera, but its impact on Romek. Being in the audience has a liberating effect on the hero. If, like the young man in *The Tram,* he has been timidly watching an attractive young woman in the train throughout the film, he is now finally able to speak to her: Romek describes the thrill of watching the spectacle.

Kieslowski acknowledged to Danusia Stok both the personal and metaphorical levels of *Personnel.* It was, among other things, a way of expressing gratitude to the College for Theater Technicians, where he first studied. (The designer who complains in the film when ornaments are added to her designs is played by his former teacher, Irena Lorentowicz.) Symbolically, "it's obvious that the film is about how we can't really find a place for ourselves in Poland," he said. "That our dreams and ideas about some ideal reality always clash somewhere along the line with something that's incomparably shallower and more wretched."[3]

Disillusionment informs Kieslowski's quietly assured first theatrical feature, *The Scar (Blizna,* 1976), as well. There are no heroes or villains in this story of the industrialization of Olecko, an impoverished Polish town, in 1970. Because bureaucrats want to "make people sit up" and stop ignoring their area, they decide to build a large chemical factory. The well-intentioned Stefan Bednarz (Franciszek Pieczka)—who had lived in Olecko with his wife twenty years earlier—is brought in to oversee the plant. It will provide needed jobs, but at the expense of both public opinion (people don't want their homes bulldozed) and the environment. Stefan dedicates himself honorably to the task and believes it will benefit the workers; they, however—concentrating on short-term goals—don't agree and he resigns.

The Scar originated in a story by journalist Romuald Karas, who co-wrote the screenplay with Kieslowski. It displays elements of both the documentary format from which Kieslowski was emerging and the poetic stylization that would characterize his later work. From the very beginning, the reality of nature itself is felt: among the trees, men in suits are comically incongruous. Later, the trees are truly cut down to make way for the plant—the scarred earth perhaps leading to the film's title. When a TV journalist then interviews Stefan on this site and his cameraman says, "This isn't fiction. No retakes," he seems to be referring to aspects of Kieslowski's methods as well. There is a documentary quality in shots of the crowd that the bureaucrats have gathered for the ministers' visit. Kieslowski's understated irony can be seen when the supportive workers leave as soon as they've been noted. The reality of the crowd is also palpable at the town meeting where older citizens complain about not being consulted.

On the other hand, there is cinematic self-awareness when Stefan arrives in his car—an exhilarating tracking shot through the town—accompanied by strange sounds as well as a synthesizer. The sounds recur four times, when he walks in the park, settles in to his new empty apartment, looks at photos of men landing on the moon, and lets his dog out of the car. As in *Curriculum Vitae,* the soundtrack functions as a tense projection of the lonely protagonist's mind. And, as in *Personnel,* a self-conscious shot invites the viewer to reflect on cinematic point of view: when Stefan tries to resign and the minister doesn't accept, they are outside on steps. Each time we look down to the other men, they seem farther away and smaller, as if being seen from a rising escalator. Are their leaders unable to speak to them on their own level?

Kieslowski's own assessment of *The Scar* was harsh: he called it

The Scar

"badly made . . . a tiny bit of socio-realism à rebours—with some socio-realistic frills even. It all takes place in factories, workshops, and at meetings . . . where socio-realists loved to film, because socio-realism didn't consider private life to be all that important."[4] The film ends with Stefan teaching his grandchild to walk, a movement from the political to the personal. Indeed, what is perhaps most interesting about *The Scar* is how it presages Kieslowski's first masterpiece, *Camera Buff*. The films share a picture-taking protagonist who is alienated from his wife, compromised by political pettiness, and finally redeemed by looking inward. Jerzy Stuhr, who plays Stefan's opportunistic assistant, would go on to star in *Camera Buff*. (Fellow director Agnieszka Holland makes a cameo appearance in *The Scar* as the secretary.)

The intervening film was *The Calm* (*Spokoj,* 1976), whose dialogue Stuhr co-wrote with Kieslowski for Polish TV. Here,

Stuhr plays Antek Gralak (the name of the protagonist in *Curriculum Vitae*), who is released from prison after serving three years. From the beginning, understated Kieslowskian irony abounds: Antek and his buddy leave jail . . . but in pouring rain. They are exhilarated at the window of the moving train . . . but a cinder lands in the friend's eye. He is happy to find again the lovely Bozena (glimpsed in flashbacks) and marry her . . . but they must live with her parents. All Antek wants, as he tells the guys at his new construction job, is peace—a wife, kids, his own place, TV after work—but this is not within his reach, especially after he is caught in a political conflict. When cement and bricks disappear from the worksite and the boss deducts the loss from their wages, the men decide to strike. Although Antek tries to mediate with the boss, his buddies beat him up. "Peace," he mutters from a bloody mouth as the film ends.

Because *The Calm* includes a strike, it was banned for many years (in *I'm So-So,* Kieslowski says three, but "six or seven years" in *Kieslowski on Kieslowski*). Nevertheless, he claimed the film "has nothing to do with politics. It simply tells the story of a man who wants very little and can't get it."[5] Once again, a documentary feeling pervades, but combined with the stylization of flashbacks, tight angles, and horse imagery. The mise-en-scène is memorably jarring when Antek is with his landlady: in the bathroom, he awkwardly gropes her sexually; later, again in the bathroom, a strained long take shows her in the foreground and him in the mirror, both aware it is their last time together.

Horses are first glimpsed in *The Calm* on a TV screen; at his wedding, Antek childishly makes clapping sounds on his body that imitate horses; from a bus at night, he sees white horses running; after he is beaten up, the image of galloping horses returns, and their sound is heard with the end credits. (A TV screen with horses also appears in *No End.*) When Kieslowski was asked in *I'm So-So* why he was drawn to horses, he replied, "they can run free." Mobility and liberty are precisely what Antek is denied in the bleak vision of *The Calm.* Moreover, he cannot have his own space, external or internal. The Polish word *pokoj* means both room and peace. And *pokoj* is indeed part of *spokoj* (calm), suggesting that you need room in order to experience calm.

Kieslowski and Stuhr's next collaboration, *Camera Buff* (*Amator,* 1979), offers a reverse scenario: Filip (Stuhr, who also co-wrote the dialogue) has achieved what Antek desired—a job, wife, child, his own apartment, and TV—but it is not enough. *Camera Buff* begins with the birth of his daughter and of his identity as a filmmaker: Filip buys an 8mm camera to record the baby and then ends up shooting beyond the domestic frame. His factory boss (Stefan Czyzewski) asks him to film the company's twenty-fifth anniversary celebration, and Filip submits the result to an amateur film festival, where his work wins a prize. To the increasing consternation of his wife Irka (Malgorzata Zabkowska), he records the world around them, from neighbors, to their changing street, to a handicapped co-worker. He even becomes an investigative reporter, thinking he will expose corruption by moving his camera through the external facade of a building to the abandoned rubble behind it. But Filip learns that there are political consequences to his choice of subject and angle. After his supportive supervisor Osuch (Jerzy Nowak) is fired and his wife leaves, Filip turns the camera on himself.

Stylistically, *Camera Buff* is Kieslowski's richest film up to 1979, its images suggesting a complex vision of the camera, the director, and the universe. (At this point, Kieslowski was thirty-eight, married, with one daughter.) It begins with a white bird attacked and killed by a dark hawk. This turns out to be the dream of Irka, who is about to give birth. While expressing her own anxious state, it also introduces a Darwinian universe—much like that of Krzysztof Zanussi's *Camouflage* (1977), which is excerpted later in *Camera Buff*. It leads us to ask, in retrospect, if the predatory relationship of hawk to bird might represent that of the filmmaker to experience. The birth that then sets the film in motion is not only of a baby but of Filip's self-awareness (the boss later says, "It's as if he'd been born with the camera"). Overcome with emotion, he hiccups in the hospital, and later at

Filip in *Camera Buff*

two other crucial moments—when his film is being shown in Lodz, and at the film's close, as he recognizes his solitude and his need to look at himself anew.

Camera Buff traces the rite of passage of a budding filmmaker from the exhilaration at capturing images to the sobering consequences. Filip begins essentially as a cameraman, recording "anything that moves," in his words. The turning point at which he becomes a director is once again expressed via bird imagery: waiting at a window for his subjects to emerge from the bathroom, he sees a pigeon fly away, places a few crumbs on the ledge, and films the returning bird. He has staged the scene. Filip's skills develop when he is told to add a verbal commentary and music to the footage he has shot. He then becomes an editor, splicing the celluloid.

But, Kieslowski suggests, technical mastery is not enough. His hero must also become a movie-goer, learning from the work of others (notably Zanussi, who appears in *Camera Buff* as himself, and the three directors about whom Filip reads in a film book— Andrzej Wajda, Karoly Makk, and Ken Loach). Filip needs to be more politically astute: when he buys a copy of the magazine *Film,* he also picks up *Politika.* In the last scene, he recounts the beginning of *Camera Buff*, thus becoming a narrator—in other words, a storyteller—who finally understands that making a film begins with the act of looking at oneself. This gaze can be quite painful, as French critic Jean Gili noted: "Kieslowski represents creation as a form of suffering, an urgency that nothing can impede, like a solitary cry before indifference or 'deals.' "[6]

An awareness of censorship—a given for Polish filmmakers—permeates *Camera Buff*, beginning with Irka asking him not to film the baby naked. The factory director buys a flashlight pen in order to note during the projection of Filip's footage what must be deleted; he later instructs him to take out three scenes—the pigeon, performers being paid, and important visitors emerging from the bathroom. Then again, to whom does the film belong? Once the plant buys the celluloid for his camera, does Filip own the work? Given that the factory director takes the prize certificate for Filip's film, probably not. This question is equally problematic when the head of the TV network (played by Boguslaw Sobczuk, a real TV producer who plays the same role in Wajda's *Man of Marble*) gives Filip film stock to shoot an exposé of corruption in his town.

While tracing the portrait of a man who ultimately loses his wife, child, and professional stability because of a passion for the camera, Kieslowski explores the varied definitions of film. It is initially a personal record, as Filip chronicles his baby's first months (which is probably quite poignant for a man who was raised in an orphanage). Irka's antagonism to the camera leads Filip to see film as an aggressive instrument: when she walks out on him, he "gives her the finger" by framing her. (This literal framing also prefigures how he will turn the camera on his own face and life at the end.) When his neighbor begs him to screen the footage Filip shot of the man's mother—who has since died—film is graphic memory that provides consolation.

Filip elevates his camera to an investigative social tool that can expose corruption when he shoots an abandoned building for which the town received construction funds. Nevertheless, he learns that his well-intentioned revelation can cause great harm, as the funds for the abandoned building were diverted to a hospital and day-care center elsewhere in the town. He therefore opens the cans, choosing to "expose" the film rather than the incident. Finally, Filip's act of turning the camera onto his own being exemplifies film's role in heightening perception, including the awareness of consequences. One can add that Osuch's cautionary tale to Filip—his brother-in-law came to a bad end at thirty, the same age as Filip, by becoming a priest!— suggests film as a form of religion.

Camera Buff contains elements of self-portraiture for Kieslowski. In *I'm So-So,* he and his friends recall how they were camera buffs themselves, and how they filmed meetings for factory bosses. Their camera? The very Krasnogorsk that Filip uses in *Camera Buff.* "I turn the camera on myself in all my films," Kieslowski adds, "but in a way that nobody can realize it." Filip's decision to destroy what he has shot echoes the director's remark upon realizing his footage could be used against people: "What a small cog I am in a wheel which is being turned by somebody else for reasons unknown to me."[7] Filip films sub-

Camera Buff

jects that Kieslowski planned to shoot himself but didn't get to do—"a documentary about pavements, or about a dwarf. Filip makes them," he acknowledged.[8]

Other personal touches include casting the "night porter" of his documentary as the man heading a gas-mask drill in the factory, and including Zanussi visiting a film club after a screening of his *Camouflage*: Filip drinks in Zanussi's wise observations that "uncertainty" is "their strength," and "criteria are relative." In addition to directing dozens of probing and inspirational motion pictures, Zanussi—as head of the TOR unit—would become one of the producers of Kieslowski's last three films.

In a 1979 interview, Kieslowski elaborated on the difference between *The Calm*, "a film about a problem," and *Camera Buff*, "a film about a character" where "humor is a manifestation of my sympathy, of sympathy for human miseries that can be funny. . . . I can identify with the camera buff."[9] But his next feature proved so problematic—especially in terms of identification—that Kieslowski ultimately kept it out of circulation. *A Short Working Day (Krotki Dzien Pracy,* 1981) takes place on June 25, 1976, the day of strikes and insurrection that led to a change in government. (In response to Gierek's raising of consumer prices, demonstrations in the industrial towns of Radom and Plock resulted in the beating and firing of thousands of workers. Poland's collapsing economy and rising dissent contributed to the tension that would culminate in Solidarity four years later.) The focus is on a First Secretary of the Communist Party (Waclaw Ulewicz), who is trying to appease the crowds of workers massing under his window. "The film is based on real events, but all the characters are fictitious," says a title card after the credits.

A Short Working Day, based on a report by Hanna Krall—who co-wrote the screenplay—opens in 1968. A young man addresses a meeting by condemning the "firebrands" who are agitating students. His call for order invokes American aggression in Vietnam and "the Israel aggression" as background. A flash-forward to 1975 shows the same man named to the prestigious Party Secretary position. By 1981, he is on television explaining his actions five years earlier. Only then does Kieslowski return to June 25, 1976, the fateful day of Polish revolt in response to the government's 69 percent price hike in meat. Structurally, this montage places the emphasis on time itself—including judgment in the future—as the measure of political activity.

The Secretary's voice-over begins when he winds the clock in his office on June 25, 1976. In these private musings, he worries and rationalizes, whereas his public utterances are confident. Holding a bullhorn, he thinks he can talk to the crowd demanding a repeal of the ludicrous price increase. But this bureaucrat is increasingly vulnerable, partly because authorities in Warsaw keep him dangling on the phone: the government is not about to give in to workers' demands. By afternoon, he must yield to the police chief's insistence that he leave his office; when he finally exits the building, the workers who have gained access are burning the furniture.

What renders *A Short Working Day* provocative is the inclusion of flash-forwards that could be "real" or imagined by the Secretary. A bearded man whistling his jeer in the crowd is caught in a freeze-frame (Kieslowski's technique mirroring that of unseen informers with cameras). We cut to a scene of the man being arrested and beaten by club-wielding policemen. A sudden return to the Secretary at his window suggests that he has imagined this retribution. Later, there is a similar freeze-frame on an older woman thrusting her puny paycheck in the Secretary's face. We cut to a trial in which she is accused of "hooliganism" before we come back to the Secretary's window.

If these are positive images for the politician, the next three flash-forwards indicate a change in the political winds. A freeze-frame once again "arrests" a red-headed man who is pulling down the Party slogan in the street. This is juxtaposed with a different young man telling the agitator's wife his group will help her obtain and pay for a lawyer. Similarly, the freeze-frame on a man with a mustache leads to a scene of him cheering the radio announcement that an agreement has been signed with the striking Gdansk workers. Finally, the flash-forward following a young man building a barricade in the street shows him broadcasting on behalf of Solidarity. Are these merely projections of the Secretary's fears or scenes that would indeed come to pass? Kieslowski seems to endorse the latter: before returning to the TV studio where the Secretary is embellishing his account in 1981, *A Short Working Day* includes black-and-white documentary footage of a rally cheering Lech Walesa—the Gdansk shipyard worker who led the 1980 strike that resulted in sweeping reforms.

As in the rest of the director's oeuvre, there are no easy villains here. Just as the domineering factory boss in *Camera Buff* is shown to have reasons for his behavior, the Party Secretary is humanized by cinematic details. Having recently quit smoking, he is constantly nibbling on candy. He is rather comic when he receives the bullhorn: "Oh shit" are the first words properly amplified, and his subsequent "ladies and gentlemen" is incongruously loud over the still-empty square. The Secretary is naive in assuming that authorities in the capital 100 kilometers away will support him. Kieslowski's approach invokes Jean Renoir's celebrated line in *Rules of the Game:* playing Octave, he laments, "There's only one terrible thing in this world, that everyone has his reasons." Kieslowski's variation in defining his own attitude was, "Even if something is happening which isn't right, even if somebody is acting badly, in my opinion, then I have to try and understand that person."[10]

He finished editing *A Short Working Day* and *Blind Chance* simultaneously, just before the imposition of martial law in 1981. Both were immediately shelved by the censors. (Because directors couldn't work during martial law, Kieslowski tried driving a taxi—in vain, since he was short-sighted and hadn't had his driver's license long enough.) By the time *A Short Working Day* could indeed be shown, he refused, calling it "boring" and "a terrible film." Perhaps he was simply fed up with politics. "At that time," he says in *I'm So-So* (referring to 1981), "I believed that politics affected us, and that we affected the political process. We had hope. We didn't realize that Communism could destroy itself. What we got is shit—a caricature of our goals." His bitter take on the Polish government goes further back to 1968, when he participated in a Lodz student strike after "they threw people out of Poland. Anti-Semitism and Polish nationalism are a stain on my country which has remained to this day and I don't think we'll ever be able to get rid of it."[11]

When *A Short Working Day* was shown on the French television station ARTE after Kieslowski's death, Vincent Amiel praised how it "deals with a recurring theme [for Kieslowski] during this period—showing a society cut in half: the bureaucratic machine is on one side, and simple citizens on the other. Whereas these two realities should express themselves and be complementary, they ignore one another at best, and then fight when a crisis breaks out."[12] It would be a mistake to assume that Kieslowski was making a film of the opposition—like, for example, Wajda with *Man of Iron*. Rather, if one is to accept his remarks on French television in 1994, film was permitting him to place germs under a microscope: "I've never belonged to the opposition, but all of us who were touched by Communism—whether we belonged to it, were against it, or indifferent like me—were infected by Communism and can't be cured. It's like AIDS, a fatal disease." His films of the 1980s would veer from overtly political material to "less tainted" psychological and metaphysical arenas.

CHAPTER THREE

Chance and Death

ALTHOUGH IT might appear from *Camera Buff* that Zanussi was the most direct influence on Kieslowski, the existential despair found in his subsequent films points more deeply to the cinematic universe of Wojciech Has. Best known for *The Saragossa Manuscript* (1964), Has is the director of haunting—and often hallucinatory—adaptations, including Bruno Schultz's *The Hour-Glass Sanatorium* (1973) and Boleslaw Prus's *The Doll* (1969), as well as tense dramas about World War II such as *How to Be Loved* (1963) and *Codes* (1966). As Richard Peña wrote in the Film Society of Lincoln Center program on the occasion of a Has retrospective in September–October 1997, this director "belongs in the tradition of the great European 'doubters'— Kafka, of course, but also Polish writers such as Bruno Schultz and Stanislaw Lem—artists who throw into question any vision of the world that marginalizes or denies the spiritual, the metaphysical or the irrational."

It is hard to ascertain how familiar Kieslowski was with the work of Has—who would become dean of the Lodz Film School in 1990—but it is likely that he saw *An Uneventful Story* (1982): Has's adaptation of Chekhov was shot by Piotr

Sobocinski—who would be Kieslowski's cinematographer for *Decalogue, 3* and *9*, as well as *Red*—and co-stars Janusz Gajos (the father in *Decalogue, 4* and Mikolaj in *White*) playing an affected fop. Both *An Uneventful Story* and Has's remarkably mature first feature *The Noose* (1958) are profoundly related to Kieslowski's work. In vision and form, these existential dramas present a bleak Poland in which the hero is doomed to cynicism and isolation. In both, Gustav Holoubek magnificently underplays the disaffected protagonist: fed up with the mediocrity of life, he can find no refuge in human contact—much like the Judge in *Red* if he had not met Valentine, or Mikolaj in *White* had he not found Karol.

The Noose (Petla) is adapted from Marek Hlasko's novel, *The First Step in the Clouds*. The stark poetic drama in compelling black-and-white chronicles the last twenty-four hours in the life of Kuba, an alcoholic trying to kick the habit but knowing he will succumb (much like Louis Malle's *Le Feu Follet* five years later). Visually, the sense of desolation—not only interior but exterior—is so extensive that we realize the problem is not just a personal one for Kuba. Post-war Poland looks like a miserable place, void of warmth or meaning. His apartment hardly seems like a home—craggy, dark walls, a lamp with a newspaper for shade, frames on the wall with no pictures, sculptures of animals made of wire lacking substance. The stylized angles increase tension: a large black telephone dominates the frame, prefiguring how it will overcome him when friends call to ask if he's really on the wagon. (A similar shot can be found toward the end of *Decalogue, 9*.)

The world outdoors is no better: a giant clock outside his window introduces both the film's emphasis on time itself as an ordeal and circular entrapment—intensified by a little girl jumping rope (perhaps the film's first "noose"). Kuba's girlfriend arrives and tells him she will pick him up at six to go to Alcoholics Anonymous, begging him to not leave the house before she returns. But out into the rain-soaked streets he goes.

High-angle shots of Kuba render him tiny and isolated, suggesting loneliness, heightened by entrapment when he is seen under telephone wires. When he accidentally meets a former love in a café, even the past is seen as encircling him.

A worker picks a fight with him and they end up at the police station, where a cop says accusingly, "I fought with the Partisans for a better Poland. Where is it? You can all go to hell." Children in the street point out to Kuba the nearest bar, where he gives himself over to double vodkas. He tells the sexy bartendress, "When you say eight, I'll kill myself today." After his seventh vodka, she says the magic word—a spiral number that encloses this film, which begins at eight one morning and ends at eight the next morning. Hope recedes as he gets increasingly drunk with another lush who tells him they can't be cured and describes the endless cycle of hospital walls. Kuba's girlfriend is waiting when he stumbles back to the apartment. Patiently, she says she will pick him up at eight the next morning. But when Kuba awakens, he finds a hidden bottle: as she arrives, he hangs himself by the window. The death of the male character, whether impending or already over, is a given in *The Noose,* as it will be in Kieslowski's *Blind Chance* and *No End.*

An Uneventful Story, while in color, tells another dark tale—that of a professor of medicine addicted to a disparaging and despairing cynicism. His own voice-over narration caustically observes how his main state is insomnia: he can no longer write nor feel love for his wife. With bitter disdain for the pettiness around him, he is on a downward slide as certain as the character Holoubek plays in *The Noose.* He pushes a poor young student out of his way into the mud; later, he is cruel to a pupil who has failed, and to another looking for a dissertation topic. Nevertheless, the sheer acuteness of his ironic glance at self and world makes him a compelling subject.

His wife forces him to check the background of their daughter's suitor (Gajos). He takes a room at an abandoned inn—the same room he occupied many years before. Katia, the only person for whom he has retained some affection, follows him there. (He and his wife raised this orphan like their own daughter.) An actress with little talent, she asks him for encouragement. But he delivers (to the camera) an existential monologue that is hopeless: because he cannot see a pattern to his existence—something beyond daily action—all it takes is a good cold to knock his mental balance. He will simply stay in this room to await what comes. The window at the heart of the screen invokes the fatal window not only of *The Noose* but also of Has's *How to Be Loved,* which ends with Zbigniew Cybulski's character jumping to a certain death.

As in much of Has's and Kieslowski's work, there is a sense of tragic waste. Shots of crows that killed two birds add to the sense of a Darwinian universe with little meaning: in painful close-ups, birds die, the head of one near the other. Is this the professor's vision? At the beginning of *An Uneventful Story,* he seems to have faith only in science; by the end, he believes in nothing. We see him lying on the bed, hands behind his head, through the bars of the headboard—a prisoner of his own intelligence and irony, probably waiting to die.

When the critic Maria Kornatowska writes about the main character of Has's *Saragossa Manuscript,* "whatever happens to him, he always finds himself in the same place, amongst the same props and settings. The only thing that he is able to gain in his illusory peregrinations is the realization of the inevitability of his destiny,"[1] she could be describing the hero of Kieslowski's *Blind Chance.* Moreover, her perception that "the window constitutes the leitmotif of Has's films," applies to Kieslowski as well. However, if the window "defines the passivity and voyeurism of the characters" in Has's work, it becomes far more dynamic in Kieslowski's cinematic vision: by the final shots of *No End, The Double Life of Veronique, Blue, White,* and *Red,* the window is a charged frame through which characters emerge into a new stage of lucidity and/or connection.

Blind Chance: Is the Script of Our Lives Already Written?

For events unfolding in the present, theater is perhaps the most fitting artistic medium. And for a story told in the past, the novel is the perfect form. Motion pictures have certainly carved out a special niche for dealing with the future; but a film like *Blind Chance (Przypadek)* suggests that the cinema is no less the quintessential medium for the "conditional" tense—what might have happened. Made in 1981 but not released until 1987, it shares with Has's films not only a concern with moral action but an investigation of the role that chance plays in our lives.

Although Kieslowski was not comfortable with the label "Cinema of Moral Anxiety" (coined by fellow filmmaker Janusz Kijowski), *Blind Chance* is a fascinating example of this very trend in post-war Polish film. And in addition to its moral exploration, the story of Witek (Boguslaw Linda) is told so provocatively that the viewer must watch carefully, constantly reassessing assumptions about political commitment, ethical behavior, free will (or destiny), and cinematic narrative. As the young hero runs to catch a train, Kieslowski presents three different versions of what might have happened to Witek: in one, he catches the train, and through a chance meeting with a dedicated Communist, joins the Party; in the second, he misses the train, fights with a guard, and ends up in the political underground; in the third, again missing the train, he returns to a quiet, apolitical life as a doctor and husband.

This intricate cinematic drama begins with a close-up of a man who suddenly screams "No": the camera then moves, quite audaciously, into the darkness of his throat for the opening credits. This man will turn out to be Witek, a medical student in the tense political climate of Poland in the late 1970s. Before the plot unfolds, we see twelve fragmentary scenes that might be Witek's flashbacks (whether lived or imagined):

1. In a hospital corridor, a body is pulled, leaving a streak of blood.
2. A little boy writes carefully as his father teaches him math.
3. The child says good-bye to his friend Daniel, who is "emigrating" to Denmark.
4. The child looks through a window where teachers are discussing students, and a bearded man reassures him.
5. The adult Witek kisses his girlfriend Czuszka, but when truckers yell obscenities, he runs after them.
6. An incision is made into a corpse, and Witek follows a fellow medical student, Olga, who leaves because she can't bear the scene.
7. His father tells him that Witek's good grades annoyed him.
8. Witek comes upon his father in a sexual embrace with his nurse.
9. Witek makes love to Olga.
10. After learning his father is dead, Witek cries uncontrollably at the train station.
11. He tells the dean of the medical school that he desires a leave.
12. Witek tries to catch the train to Warsaw, which is already departing the station.

In many of these scenes, the point of view initially seems to be subjective—from Witek's eyes—but the camera then reveals him within the frame. This visual strategy not only underlines the omniscience of the camera as narrator but also makes us aware of the partiality of our perception. For example, little Witek learning math is initially seen in the mirror, but the camera moves to reveal the reflection and the larger frame. Similarly, the angle is extremely low when he reaches for his girlfriend Czuszka, but this point-of-view shot then includes him as perceived rather than merely perceiver. "You'd better be on your toes," Kieslowski seems to be saying to the audience.

Blind Chance

As Witek runs madly for the train, he knocks into an older woman (taking the time to apologize) who drops some change. One coin rolls to the foot of a scruffy-looking man, who picks it up and buys himself a beer. Like the two-franc coin that will seem to stick to Karol's palm in *White,* this coin might symbolize chance—or fate—as Witek jostles the man before sprinting onto the platform. (Only in the second version, however, does Witek knock the glass out of his hand.)

Witek's essential decency and courage manifest themselves as soon as he boards the train: noting that a long-haired young man is in police custody, he tries to help him escape the train—only to be rebuffed. In the Communist veteran Werner (Tadeusz Lomnicki), however, Witek finds a kindred idealistic spirit. Werner, who takes the young man to his Warsaw apartment, explains that he was imprisoned as "a deviationist" and released in 1954. He introduces Witek to Adam (Zbigniew Zapasiewicz), a Communist Party functionary. Believing he can improve the world by working within the system, Witek joins the Party—to the anger of Czuszka (Boguslawa Pawelec), whom he has met again by chance.

Jerzy Stuhr, in a role quite opposite from *Camera Buff,* plays a Party official who seizes the opportunity to send Witek in his place to a problem site: Witek is to stop the "mutiny" unfolding at a drug treatment hospital where the Party has replaced the doctors with its own staff. Witek tries to mediate, but the young rebels who have taken over the hospital (including the long-haired guy from the train) are intransigent. They have locked doctors into a cage—from which Witek surreptitiously releases them. They put Witek in the cage, and threaten to burn him alive . . . but do not. After Czuszka is arrested—presumably because Adam knows of her activities from Witek—our hero attacks Adam. He then arrives at the airport, where a group of Poles are to travel to Paris. But before boarding, they are told they cannot leave because strikes are breaking out in Poland.

The second version begins with Witek missing the train, fighting with a guard, being arrested and sentenced to thirty days of community service. He thus meets Marek (Jacek Borkowski) and is invited into the dissident circle. Witek brings to this group the same dedication he manifested in the first section. But his political commitment here is blended with religious calling, partly through contact with the character of the priest Stefan (Adam Ferency), a wheelchair-bound activist. Witek is baptized, ironically at the same time that he embarks upon an affair with a married Jewish woman: Vera (Marzena Trybala) is the sister of Daniel, his boyhood friend who was forced to emigrate in the late 1960s.

Witek is sent to the home of a woman just after it is ransacked by government thugs. With remarkable calm, she explains to Witek that she is afraid of nothing: doctors told her twelve years ago that she had only three years to live. "Life is a gift," she concludes, and quotes Mother Teresa about the one thing you can give someone who is dying—"the belief that you are not completely alone." Her perception recalls Werner's lecture in a class during the first version: Werner admits that even though the beacon of hope has been receding continually, life is a sorry experience for those without hope. (Kieslowski winks at the audience toward the end of the second version when Witek asks a man for directions at the station: it is the Communist Werner.)

At one point, Witek is supposed to go to Paris for a conference but is told that he will be given a visa only if he provides names to the government. Consequently, he will not go to France. The segment ends with Witek's despair upon learning from Marek that authorities found their secret printing basement and arrested their colleagues.

In the third version, Witek misses the train, returns to Warsaw, marries Olga (Monika Gozdzik), and returns to medicine. He refuses to join the Party but is no less resistant to dissident petitions and to religion. The dean of the medical school asks Witek to take his place on a plane to Libya for a medical conference; he accepts, and changes the flight in order to be with Olga for her birthday. He will therefore have to travel via Paris.

At the airport, the camera reveals to the viewer two elements of which Witek is ignorant: a female airline attendant from Part I carries documents for the Communist Party group, and Stefan from Part II waits for the same flight. In other words, this is the very plane that Witek was supposed to take in the two previous versions. Just after takeoff, the plane explodes into flames.

In retrospect, the film opens with the primal scream of Witek a moment before his plane crashes. Images of the past flash before his eyes—except, perhaps, for the first shot in the hospital corridor: while it might be the scene of his birth (the shot is repeated when he describes being born to Czuszka), it could also be the scene of his death.

Why does Witek die in the third version only? Is Kieslowski suggesting that an apolitical life is tantamount to death? Or is his life like the "Slinky" toy that Werner shows him in Part I? Witek and Werner marvel at how the mechanism moves down the stairs according to its own rhythm. But when it reaches the ground floor, Witek remarks that its stasis is like death.

The "Slinky" is one of the many quirky details that inform *Blind Chance,* surprising the viewer with unexpected twists. At the beginning, Witek's father says he preferred when his son got bad grades; later, Werner admits to having wanted to touch a beloved woman precisely because of the fuzz on her upper lip and her ugly, pudgy hands. After Czuszka and Witek make love in Warsaw, she holds a lit cigarette over his sleeping head, creating tension as we fear the ash will fall on him: then she flicks it on his face. Before becoming baptized, he stares at a garishly commercial Christ figure whose eyes open and close. In Part III, he visits a dying woman and then notices her younger relatives juggling intricately—indeed professionally—in the backyard. These idiosyncratic details add vivid life to a film that moves inexorably toward death.

In a sense, Witek dies because he takes the place of the dean. This fulfills a pattern of displacement that Kieslowski develops throughout *Blind Chance.* The aging Werner takes the place of Witek's dead father. Witek substitutes for the doctors in the cage. And he is perhaps taking the place of his twin brother who died at birth (like the French Veronique who continues after the Polish Veronika dies in mid-song). If, as he tells his girlfriend, he survived birth because he emerged just before his brother, there is an analogy in the situation of Werner and Adam: it was Adam who got out of prison before him, and who therefore married their beloved Krystyna—in addition to establishing a foothold in the political hierarchy.

The fact that we see three versions rather than two means it is not a simple choice of one way of life versus another; rather, it is open-ended, for where three versions exist, there can be four or more. Indeed, Alain Masson cleverly referred to the construction of *Blind Chance* as "a dilemma, or rather a trilemma."[2] Kieslowski invites the audience to ponder whether Witek's experiences derive from choice, chance, or destiny. As he said in *I'm So-So,* "We are a sum of several things, including

Werner and Witek in *Blind Chance*

individual will, fate (but we can change fate a little), and chance, which is not so important. It's the path we choose that is crucial." Unlike dialectical (or socio-political) materialism, *Blind Chance* posits a belief in a moral core as well as accidental or external conditions. It is precisely because his father has told him, "you are under no obligation," that he commits to political action in Parts I and II. Witek behaves decently in all three episodes but is killed anyway in the one where he seems least bound to ideology and most content.

Blind Chance is not merely a rich cinematic experience on its own terms. It also seems to be the basis for *Sliding Doors* (1998), a British first feature written and directed by Peter Howitt. This reduced transposition of *Blind Chance* and *The Double Life of Veronique* offers two versions instead of three: if Helen (Gwyneth Paltrow) catches the London subway, she will meet James (John Hannah) and come home in time to find her boyfriend Jerry (John Lynch) in bed with Lydia (Jeanne Tripplehorn). If she misses the train, she will hail a cab, be mugged, and have to go to the hospital—getting home just after Lydia's departure.

Sliding Doors crosscuts the two versions, both of which culminate in a pregnant Helen being hit by a car. The one who met James will die; the other Helen will emerge from the same hospital where James is visiting his mother: at the end, they will meet anyway, as if fated. Whereas Kieslowski layers his "what if?" stories with poetic and political dimensions, *Sliding Doors* flattens possibilities: the only concerns are romance and whether Helen will continue to work in public relations.

More significantly, *Blind Chance* is a prefiguration of the *Three Colors* trilogy. The triadic structure links the two works, as does the notion of uniting major characters at the end for an accident. In *Blind Chance,* they probably die; at the end of the trilogy, the three couples from *Blue, White,* and *Red* are saved. Perhaps they learn one of the precepts of *Blind Chance:* "Life is a gift," says the woman who was given three years to live and has survived twelve. Indeed, Witek's life—given that his twin brother died at birth—has been a gift. Because the film's action begins when Witek becomes an orphan, *Blind Chance* can be related to *Camera Buff,* whose protagonist was raised in an orphanage. And if the death of the father propels Witek's story, the death of the husband will set in motion the tale of *No End.*

No End: Incorporating a Ghost

No End (*Bez Konca*) marks the beginning of two seminal relationships for Kieslowski: composer Zbigniew Preisner and writer Krzysztof Piesiewicz would continue to collaborate with the director on all his subsequent work. Preisner, a musician with the famous Kraków underground cabaret *Pivnica Pod Baranami* (The Cellar Under the Rams), had scored only one film before meeting Kieslowski. For *No End,* he composed a spare, haunting score, whose central melody would become the core of the soundtrack for *Blue.* Kieslowski met Piesiewicz, a defense lawyer, while trying to film political trials in 1982. The atmosphere in Poland at the time was one of intimidation that

No End

Kieslowski found ludicrous, especially with courts passing long sentences for trivial matters. It was enough to be caught with an underground newspaper or on the street past curfew to be sentenced, and someone painting political graffiti could be given three years in jail.

Although Piesiewicz did not trust the filmmaker at first, and the authorities were reluctant to permit courtroom shooting, Kieslowski was finally given access to both public and military courts. "Piesiewicz agreed, in the names of some of his clients, to the filming," Kieslowski recalled.

> The moment I started shooting, something strange began to happen. The judges didn't sentence the accused. That is, they passed some sort of deferred sentences which weren't, in fact, at all painful. . . . The judges didn't want to be recorded at the moment of passing unjust sentences, because they knew that if I turned on the camera, then some time in the future, after 3, 10 or 20 years, somebody would find this film.[3]

Consequently, he would go into courtrooms even if his camera contained no film: "They were simply dummy cameras which were only there so that through plain human fear, the judges wouldn't pass sentences." Although Kieslowski attended over fifty trials in this manner, cinematically "nothing came of it."

This background feeds into *No End* (1984), simultaneously a political drama, a ghost story, and a somber meditation on romantic love. It takes place in 1982 during martial law and develops tensions from *Blind Chance*—whether chance versus fate, or political activism versus pragmatic humanism. The film opens with a high-angle shot of a cemetery, an omniscient (divine?) point of view that shows candles flickering above graves. There is a cut to a man's hand, disembodied, then the blurred reflection of his face, and finally the full figure of Antek (Jerzy Radziwillowicz) is revealed.[4] He sits down and addresses the audience in a monologue: he died a few days earlier of a heart attack, peacefully, and is now seated beside the sleeping body of his wife Urszula (Grazyna Szapolowska). When the distraught widow awakens, she cannot see what the camera's movement reveals—that Antek is watching her.

This highly respected lawyer was defending Darek (Artur

Antek in *No End*

Barcis), a young man who started a strike in a factory. Darek's wife Joanna (Maria Pakulnis) pleads with Urszula to help her get a substitute lawyer. She recommends Antek's former professor Labrador (Aleksander Bardini), who reluctantly accepts the case. Darek's aims are not identical to his new lawyer's: whereas the pragmatic and weary Labrador wants to free him, the prisoner is concerned with principles—or with protecting his honor. He sees no difference between compromise and selling out. In the final courtroom scene, it is hard to decipher whether they have won or lost: the judge finds Darek guilty, but the eighteen-month sentence is suspended for two years.

Urszula deals with her increasingly painful loss. Although she has her kind son Jacek and her work as a translator (of George Orwell), she realizes how much she misses Antek. Urszula even tries hypnosis with an earnest young practitioner (Tadeusz Bradecki); but instead of making her forget Antek, the session leads to Urszula seeing her husband clearly before her. After taking Jacek to his grandmother's house, she methodically seals the vents, opens the gas (the camera moves into the blackness of the stove—like the darkness of Witek's throat in the first shot of *Blind Chance*—then out again), and kills herself. In the last shot, she is joined by Antek, and they walk away together.

The beginning of *No End* feels like a continuation of Kieslowski's previous film: had the decent Witek of *Blind Chance* become a lawyer rather than a doctor—and died—these might be the wife and child he left behind. But as the film progresses, its internal coherence is more compelling than its possible origins in "the triple life of Witek." The opening and closing scenes of *No End* are symmetrically linked by a movement from light to dark and back. The cemetery lit by candles is suddenly black—abstracted, with only the flickering lights—and then a cut to morning brings the tombs back into view. In this manner, Kieslowski introduces time as a palpable presence. This continues when the disembodied voice on a phone in Antek's house announces 7:20 A.M., followed by the ghost telling us that he died four days earlier. Later, when Labrador drops his pocket watch, time stops literally as well as figuratively: not only does this gift from Antek cease working, but Labrador then learns that mandatory retirement has been instituted for those above seventy (which motivates him to accept Darek's case). The aging lawyer is subsequently seen as a small figure in the background, the foreground including the edge of a giant clock.

Politically, time is invoked directly when Darek receives a suspended sentence: although he is to be imprisoned for eighteen months, it will be two years before he has to serve! Finally, Urszula's death is a matter of patience: instead of sticking her head in the oven (like the movement of the camera), she sits before the stove, waiting peacefully for the gas to come to her. When she is reunited with her husband, it seems as if he were waiting for her.

Even as a ghost, Antek makes his mark throughout *No End*. This is literally the case when Urszula finds a question mark next to Labrador's name in a directory on her husband's desk—although it was absent from the page when Antek died. (Indeed, when she tells Darek's wife that Antek made the mark, Joanna doesn't question it.) Moreover, the dog seems to feel Antek's presence. And in a mesmerizing scene, one wonders whether he is protecting his wife: Urszula's car stops on a road; another automobile passes; her car starts again; she finds that the other one just collided with a bus. Chance? Fate? Or the intervention of the angelic ghost? Even if Antek is not seen on this road, perhaps he is enabling her to choose a peaceful death rather than succumb to a violent one. In any case, the passing car has taken the place of Urszula's, just as Witek in *Blind Chance* took the dean's place in the doomed plane.

Rather, Antek is revealed in surprising moments, like the scene in which Urszula allows herself to be picked up by a young British stranger. When she removes her clothes in his hotel bathroom, the camera reframes to show Antek—incorporating him in both senses of inclusion and corporeal substance. After she has sex with this man (who mistakes her for a hooker), she doesn't need to see her husband in order to be overwhelmed by his presence: making sure the stranger speaks no Polish, she embarks on a monologue about Antek. What she can't bear now, Urszula explains, is that she did not appreciate at the time how happy she was with her husband.

Why, in her grief, has she allowed for this fleeting seduction? Because the ardent British visitor's hands reminded her of Antek's. Hands are central to *No End,* beginning with the ghost's abstracted fingers: this image introduces hands that have no agency—an impotence like that of Urszula's fingers in close-up playing frustratedly with her stockinged toes until the hose tears. The shadow of Antek's hand passes over his son's sleeping body and then touches gently the back of the boy's neck.

The delicately understated expression of Urszula's loss is first expressed in a close-up of her hands: she automatically makes two glasses of coffee, suddenly stops, and throws one out. The same glass shape returns in the session with the hypnotist: she sees Antek moving his finger on the rim of the empty glass, making a hypnotic sound of his own. She subsequently holds a

Urszula in *No End*

glass of coffee in her kitchen: in close-up we watch the glass slip slowly down and finally crash on the floor.

Hands that are unable to touch or hold inform Kieslowski's larger theme: *No End* takes to its ultimate limit the notion of man's inability to do anything. We feel that Antek is not made for these times. On the other hand, the concrete presence of this ghost conveys the director's metaphysical belief in how the dead continue inside the living:

> I do think there's a need within us—not only a need but also a fundamental kind of feeling—to believe that those who have gone and whom we dearly loved, who were important to us, are constantly within or around us. . . . I mean that they exist within us as somebody who judges us and that we take their opinions into account even though they're dead. I very often have the feeling that my father is somewhere nearby. It doesn't matter if he's actually there or not, but if I wonder what he'd say about what I've done or want to do, that means he's there. My mother, too.[5]

The very movement of the camera in the last scene suggests that Urszula is not alone in her moment of death. In retrospect, the opening high angle of the cemetery might be Antek's point of view, a Wendersian (as in *Wings of Desire*) kind of angel who cares—if powerlessly—for those below. And throughout *No End,* the camera placement and movement are dramatically used. Antek addresses it directly (like Filip in the last scene of *Camera Buff*); similarly, Urszula toward the end lights matches and says "I love you" to the camera representing Antek. He is first glimpsed in the glass of their library, but the camera leaves ambiguous whether he walks behind it or is reflected within it. Likewise, the last shot seems to be a reflection of the ghosts, from the back, receding from our view. Kieslowski could have run the final credits on a black screen, as most films do; but they unfold on the image of the reunited lovers, stilled less by death than by the camera's freeze-frame. This fulfills his definition of

No End

the film's close as a happy one; indeed, the original title of *No End* was *Happy End*.

The soundtrack is equally expressive. The mournful voices in song provide a sound bridge from the cemetery to Antek's home—followed by the ominous recording on the phone that intones, "this call is being monitored," before we hear the time. Urszula's encounter with the car accident is accompanied by the repetition of the other auto's horn, even after the crash: in an eerie manner, the car—although "dead"—continues to emit sound. When she looks jealously through her husband's things after meeting a woman he knew in his youth, screeching strings accompany her search. They return, embedded in Preisner's music, when she has sex with the stranger.

The edginess provided by the soundtrack—consisting of both diegetic (emanating within the frame) and nondiegetic (external) sources—ultimately expresses the political climate of the film. Even if Kieslowski's sympathy is with the suffering widow and beloved ghost, *No End* is equally concerned with the complex judicial game that Darek and Labrador play out. The lawyer uses a surgical metaphor in explaining to Joanna his plan—to take the scalpel and hack away—because his aim is to save a life. Darek, on the other hand, is like a cowboy hero in American westerns—concerned with his sense of honor, especially in the showdown. An intransigent idealist, he is hardly "the hero" in whom the hope for a new Poland might lie. On Kieslowski's political spectrum, Antek seems to be in the middle: he is less resigned than Labrador, more flexible than Darek. But he is dead, thereby thwarting audience complacency: there is no single hero in *No End*. Rather, as the director put it, "I thought . . . that martial law was really a defeat for everyone, that everyone lost, that during martial law we all bowed our heads."[6]

The result was a negative reception by all of Poland's central organizations—the government, the opposition (because *No End* showed defeat), and the Church. "We really got a thrashing over it," Kieslowski admitted. "Only one element didn't give us a thrashing, and that was the audience."[7] His disillusionment with politics would continue throughout the 1980s, even if it was no longer an explicit cinematic theme. During an interview at the 1989 Montreal Film Festival, for example, Kieslowski saw no point in giving opinions about the government: "The day I can buy toilet paper in a Polish store, I'll discuss politics," he proposed drily. "The political situation is changing very quickly, maybe too fast. We'll probably have to pay for this rapid transformation. Years will go by before changes from the top affect the bottom of daily life."[8]

CHAPTER FOUR

The Decalogue—Ten Short Films

About Mortality

A decade ago, Krzysztof Kieslowski made his 10-part cycle of
short films, which dramatize the Ten Commandments in modern Poland. In their scope, wit, power and ethical poignancy,
they stand even taller today.

—Richard Corliss, in naming *The Decalogue* number 2
of his Ten Best Films of 1998, *Time Magazine*[1]

ALTHOUGH MADE as a ten-part series for Polish Television in
1988–9, *The Decalogue* is an extraordinary cinematic achievement. Whether applauded at film festivals from Venice to San
Sebastian, or heavily attended during a theatrical run in Paris,
these one-hour dramatizations loosely based on the Ten Commandments catapulted Kieslowski into the international lime-
light. The idea originated with Krzysztof Piesiewicz in the early
1980s, and many of the situations derive from his legal or personal experiences. For example, Piesiewicz revealed about
Decalogue, 1, "One day my son, who was 12, didn't return from
ice-skating when he was supposed to. Moreover, my cousin is a
physics professor in Philadelphia whose son is so brilliant that
his father sometimes doesn't understand what he says. I unified
the two elements to imagine this story."[2]

They embarked on the project at a time when Kieslowski's
perception of life was dour:

Chaos and disorder ruled Poland in the mid-1980s—every-
where, everything, practically everybody's life. Tension, a
feeling of hopelessness, and a fear of yet worse to come were

obvious. I'd already started to travel abroad a bit by this time and observed a general uncertainty in the world at large. I'm not even thinking about politics here but about ordinary, everyday life. I sensed mutual indifference behind polite smiles and had the overwhelming impression that, more and more frequently, I was watching people who didn't really know why they were living. So I thought Piesiewicz was right, but filming the Ten Commandments would be a very difficult task.[3]

Over a little more than a year, they wrote the screenplays, intending to parcel them out to ten different directors. "But I liked doing the first film so much," Kieslowski admitted, "that I didn't want to give the others away."[4] The result was that he shot and edited all ten over a twenty-one-month period, using different cinematographers for each episode.[5] He would occasionally shoot parts of one film in the morning, of a second at another location in the afternoon, and of a third in the evening. When asked to compare directing for television with the big screen, he replied, "The only difference is that TV pays you less and you have to work faster. I treat both forms in the same way—and perhaps TV even more seriously: if you come into someone's home, you have to behave."[6] Despite ludicrously short rehearsal time and limited film stock (his shooting ratio was 2:1), Kieslowski enlisted a remarkable cast, blending stars like Daniel Olbrychski and Krystyna Janda with unknown actors.

The director's sardonic tone coexists with a compassionate eye for his characters' fumbling and often deluded attempts at living happily. Linked by a Warsaw apartment complex, they enact dramas of moral choice. As he says in the introduction to the published script, "I believe the life of every person is worthy of scrutiny, containing its own secrets and dramas."[7]

Each of the stories is preceded by a number rather than a commandment. But when *The Decalogue* was presented at the 1989 Venice Film Festival, the press office was deluged by critics' questions about the specific commandment to which each episode was linked. After a few days, the press office published a list of titles—an addition to the series rather than something Kieslowski intended.[8] "Some of my actors who were religious didn't want to act in the 'Decalogue' unless I told them which commandment it was about," he remarked. "But this is really not important. One can exchange the . . . sixth with the ninth, the fourth with the seventh."[9] In fact, *9* and *10* seem to share the ninth commandment—"Thou shalt not covet thy neighbor's house . . . thy neighbor's wife . . . nor any thing that is thy neighbor's"—while the annotated list leaves out the second commandment, "Thou shalt not make unto thee any graven image." Rather than asking us to be literal-minded, *The Decalogue* provokes contemplation of how the spirit of the Commandments might still be applicable to our daily lives.

Decalogue, 1

In *1,* Pawel (Wojciech Klata) is the brilliant and loving son of Krzysztof (Henryk Baranowski[10]), a kind professor who believes in logic, science, and his computer. After seeing a dead dog, Pawel asks his father about death. He answers simply that the heart stops pumping. Whereas the professor believes "there is no soul," his sister Irena (Maja Komorowska) is a devout Catholic who tries to share her faith with Pawel. When the boy (who is approximately eleven years old) asks her about God, she hugs him and replies that He is in the love of their embrace.

Father and son happily calculate via computer that the ice has frozen enough for Pawel to go skating on the lake. But when the boy doesn't come home, Krzysztof realizes that the sirens and crowd by the lake mean that Pawel is lost below the ice. Although the published script ends with Krzysztof in a church after interrogating his computer in vain, the film closes with him holding a piece of ice (from holy water) to his head, and a shot of Pawel on a television screen: a TV crew had been at his school, and this image is what remains of the boy—a freeze-frame, visually recalling the television screen glimpsed by his aunt in the film's second scene.

The father in *Decalogue, 1*

The first *Decalogue* episode presents one of life's most unfathomable and inconsolable occurrences—the death of a child. Kieslowski thus begins the series on a note of gravity that takes the viewer beyond expectations of entertainment. (The possible destruction of a child is a theme that recurs throughout *The Decalogue,* notably in episodes *2, 5, 7,* and *8*.) His philosophical probing and formal mastery eschew sentimentality, inviting a truly thoughtful engagement on the audience's part. What, indeed, are we to make of the fact that Krzysztof's computer has apparently switched on by itself early in the film, while Pawel's computer does the same after the child is dead? Both read (in English), "I am ready." For commands? For life? For death?

Screens, like other surfaces, are full of mysteries in *1*. The first shot—a frozen lake—can be likened to the TV screen in the second scene: we don't know what lies under the surface. But by the end, the lake has been shown to contain death by keeping the child within its melted water; the television is no longer a simple screen but maintains the child "alive" within it. And, as Joel Magny elaborates in his perceptive essay, "*Decalogue, 1:* Fire and Ice," the insertion of the TV screen at the beginning renders what follows "an immense flashback. What we witness has already taken place, ineluctably."[11] Kieslowski thus creates the illusion of fatality.

The published screenplay is fascinating precisely because it is not a shooting script but a blueprint. The changes made by Kieslowski from the screenplay to the final movie tend to replace literal details with suggestive images. For example, the script of *1* begins with the apartment block in late autumn: "A mongrel bitch is being chased by several male dogs. Owners of cars parked in the alleyways emerge from the stairwells carrying batteries. . . . "[12] The film, on the contrary, opens with a shot of the frozen lake, suggesting winter. The camera surveys this elemental image, void of human habitation, depicting a desolate universe. We then see a young man (Artur Barcis, who played the intransigent defendant in *No End*) seated beside a smoking fire. He is part of this landscape, the furry collar of his coat adding a primitive, animal look. The solitary figure looks enigmatically at the camera.

We will never know exactly who he is, but this man is seen at least four more times in *1* and returns throughout *The Decalogue.* Like Antek's ghost in *No End,* his presence can be connected to that of the angels in Wim Wenders's *Wings of Desire:* they are pure "gaze," able—like a film camera (or director?)—to record human folly and suffering but unable to alter the course of the lives they witness. Kieslowski observed, "He has no influence on the action, but he leads the characters to think about what they are doing. . . . His intense stare engenders self-examination."[13]

In scene two, Irena looks at the television in the street at night and, seeing Pawel's face—in slow motion before freeze-frames that graphically invoke an arrested life—sheds a tear. A cut to the young man by the fire shows him wiping away a tear. It is only at this point that *1* rejoins the screenplay, as a pigeon alights on a window which turns out to be Pawel's—like Kieslowski selecting this story among others that could be told in the same apartment complex. (Reminiscent of Filip in *Camera Buff*, Pawel has attracted the pigeon with crumbs. And like the birds that open *Camera Buff*, Pawel's pigeon suggests danger: spots of blood can be glimpsed on its side.)

The young man (whom we will call the "angel") is subsequently shown following a shot of the church; after Irena defines God to Pawel; following the scene of the boy visiting his father's class; and when Krzysztof goes out at night to verify whether the ice is solid enough. At this point, he sees the "angel" beside the flames. Later, when the police search for bodies in the broken lake, Krzysztof notices the fire . . . but the young man is conspicuously absent. Since the film leaves out a significant line from the screenplay—that the power station released some hot water into the lake during the night (p. 24)—one wonders whether the fire of the "angel" might have contributed to the accident.

Kieslowski provides no easy answer. When the ice turns out to be fatally weak, the commandment on which the episode is loosely based assumes a derisive poignancy: "Thou shalt have no other Gods but me." As the director said:

> The God of the Old Testament is a demanding, cruel God; a God who doesn't forgive, who ruthlessly demands obedience to the principles which He has laid down. . . . [He] leaves us a lot of freedom and responsibility, observes how we use it and then rewards or punishes, and there's no appeal or forgiveness. It's something which is lasting, absolute, evident and is not relative. And that's what a point of reference must be, especially for people like me, who are weak, who are looking for something, who don't know.[14]

Are these characters punished for an excessive faith in technology or mathematics? Pawel is, after all, a computer wiz, proudly showing Irena how he can open doors or water faucets with a flick of the keys. This illusion of control has its limitations, however; while he is able to program/deduce what his mother might be doing on her trip far away—like sleeping—the computer cannot answer when he types in the question, "What does she dream?"[15]

Krzysztof is surprised that the computer seems to have switched on by itself. But Kieslowski deleted the crucial penultimate scene in which the distraught father searches for answers beyond the machine's capability:

KRZYSZTOF: Are you there?
(Despite the fact that Krzysztof has pressed the reply command button, the computer thinks for a moment, and then a sentence appears.)
COMPUTER: *(In English)* Repeat again.
KRZYSZTOF: I asked if you were there.
(The computer is silent. Krzysztof presses the key with the request for a response, but the screen merely glows with the same bright, green light. After a while Krzysztof again taps out some more letters, one after the other.)
What can I do?
(The question remains on screen for a moment, then the screen goes green again and the letters disappear. Krzysztof types out a further question.)
Why?
(As before, the letters dissolve into greenness. Krzysztof's hands continue to to punch out the keys on the keyboard.)
Why take a small boy?
(The sentence lingers. Krzysztof adds another one.)
Listen to me. Why take a small boy? I want to understand.
(He presses the reply key—the letters disappear. He continues to write.)
If you are there, give me a sign.
(The sentence lingers. Krzysztof deletes the first letters of the sentence. They disappear one after the other, leaving only one word remaining: 'Sign.' He presses the key several times again, and finally the word occupies the whole screen: 'Sign.' He presses the command key 'answer'. The computer quickly responds.)

Computer: Manifestation. Omen. Mark. Symbol.
(Krzysztof writes.)
KRZYSZTOF: Illumination.
COMPUTER: Light. Fire. Beam. Candle.
(The computer is now responding swiftly. Krzysztof writes.)
KRZYSZTOF: Candle.
COMPUTER: Symbol. Church. Cross.
(Krzysztof writes on.)
KRZYSZTOF: Sense. Hope.
(The computer falls silent for a moment. Then letters start to appear.)
COMPUTER: (In English) Terminology unrecognized. (pp. 27–8)

Kieslowski substitutes other images that carry narrative weight. For example, Krzysztof is upset by ink that suddenly and inexplicably stains his papers. Since, in retrospect, this occurs at the very moment Pawel is on the ice, it functions as a foreboding: liquid is out of control. (And how appropriate that Krzysztof is confronted by ink—the former "matter" of written language—when he is so dependent on the inkless computer.) Liquid permeates *Decalogue, 1* in a number of suggestive forms, including milk (Pawel brings home a bottle, but it has turned sour; the TV crew has come to his school because of its milk program; the frozen milk bottle alerts father and son to icy temperature for skating), ice, and tears. This imagery culminates in the scene of Krzysztof entering an empty church, knocking over the altar, and causing the candles to fall. The wax drips down a painting of the Virgin Mary, creating a strikingly appropriate image of tears—which recall those of the aunt and the "angel" in the first scene. As Columbia student Marie Regan wrote in an unpublished manuscript:

In Poland, where Mary is the central icon of Catholicism, it seems telling to reassert her image as a grieving mother. Her story, and that of Christianity, is that of the sacrificed child to a greater cause. . . . Krzysztof reaches—in what might be an unconscious repetition of a childhood ritual of belief—to the holy water for blessing. The water is frozen into a circle, not unlike the host/wafer of communion. Krzysztof raises the ice to his forehead, the place of his memory and reason, as he struggles to understand his loss.

The Decalogue thus leads us to experience the realm of the symbolic occupied by both art and religion.

Pawel and his aunt in *Decalogue, 1*

In the screenplay, the church is filled with people. But Kies-lowski deleted even the priest from this scene. Instead, a sense of cosmic loneliness prevails. By this point, we have already seen the frightened Krzysztof in the elevator with an old man—who offers no greeting—and running after the parents of Pawel's friend: they cruelly refuse to stop in order for their son to tell Krzysztof that Pawel was not playing with him.

As in *Blind Chance* and *No End,* a decent character with everything to live for dies. Kieslowski does not presume to offer answers, but he includes a resonant phrase: "Being alive is a gift," Irena tells Pawel, echoing what the older woman told Witek in Part II of *Blind Chance.* Life is a present, presumably even if that life is short.

Decalogue, 2

The gift of being alive is at the heart of *Decalogue, 2,* which centers on a violinist, Dorota (Krystyna Janda), whose husband is dying in the nearby hospital. She asks the doctor (Aleksander Bardini)—who lives in her building—whether he might survive; the aged physician cannot answer. She finally explains that she must know because, after seeming infertile, she is pregnant with another man's child and will abort only if her husband Andrzej recovers.

Heightened imagery expresses the characters and their situations. Death is invoked in the opening scene, as a caretaker finds a dead rabbit that fell from a window. He knocks on the doctor's door, thinking it belongs to him. The physician says no and goes back to the "hothouse" he has created on his balcony: the cactus plant he tends is appropriate to the prickly temperament not only of the doctor but of Dorota. In her initial interactions with him, they are unsmiling and downright thorny. She asks if he remembers her. "Yes, you ran over my dog two years ago," he recalls drily. If the doctor hopes to save his cactus, Dorota picks leaves off a plant in her apartment and then tries to break the stem. But it moves back up of its own accord, suggesting the life force that will reanimate her husband. (The fact that the leaves reappear in his hospital room suggests that her action may not have been as destructive as it seemed: Dorota might have removed them for her husband.)

With simplicity and economy, Kieslowski tells us a great deal about these characters. The doctor is cosmopolitan—he listens to radio news in English—but lives modestly and walks to the hospital. Like the character Janda played in Wajda's *Man of Marble,* Dorota is a chain-smoker, each cigarette externalizing her edgy energy. When there is no ashtray at the doctor's apartment, she flicks into her matchbox, which then flares symbolically when she must put the cigarette out. Photos on her wall indicate that her husband is a mountain climber—who perhaps leaves her alone for long periods—while her lover's messages on the answering machine establish that he is a musician. Elegant clothes and the click of her high heels suggest that a violinist with the Philharmonic earns more than a doctor. Nevertheless, both must resort to boiling water if they want to take baths: there is no hot water in the building.

Liquid and glass are central images in *Decalogue, 2.* If Urszula in *No End* let slip from her hand a glass of tea or coffee that shattered on the kitchen floor, Dorota sits by the kitchen table beside a full glass on a saucer: she slowly and methodically pushes them to the edge, and they fall to the ground. Instead of being able to contain and proffer warmth, the glass becomes an emblem of fragility, as likely to break as the heroines. Liquid is ominous in the hospital as well, where the husband's point of view shows relentless dripping of the walls (recalling the drops of sweat on his face). We also see water plopping into the bloody bedpan, a graphic embodiment of slow-moving time.

These images converge in the glass of stewed fruit that Dorota brings to the hospital. Although we never see it opened or consumed, a panning shot from the finally recovering husband to the glass ends with a close-up of a bee working its way out of the fruit to the top of the spoon. The bee struggles to survive above a glass whose contents now resemble the bloody

Dorota in *Decalogue, 2*

bedpan: most of the berries are gone, and it seems as if dripping water has refilled the glass.

Like the plant stem, the bee's life force is of course symbolic of the husband's, whose recovery is nothing short of miraculous. The doctor believes he has little chance of survival at the outset; then, the patient seems to improve a bit; but because Dorota is about to have an abortion, the doctor swears to her that he will die. She therefore keeps the child. The doctor thus saves two lives rather than one, and we see connections to both his own life and to *Decalogue, 1*. On two occasions, over a glass of coffee, he recounts to his cleaning lady a story about a family—all killed during World War II—that turns out to have been his own. When Dorota's husband tells him at the end that he is very happy they will have a child, Kieslowski adds two lines that are not in the published script: "Do you know what it is to have children?" asks the patient. "Yes, I know," answers the doctor. As in *1*, we are left with a father who has lost a child; but in a sense, the patient "balances" the loss as he looks forward to the miracle of a baby.

This ending foregrounds the doctor's own story, and brings us back to the moment when Dorota is about to enter the doctor's apartment: he turns to the wall a photo of his wife and children. In this manner, we see and respect the doctor's need for privacy—for not sharing his grief with strangers like this nervous neighbor. Similarly, when she asks if he believes in God, he replies that he has "a private God." Kieslowski echoes his character's sentiment in *I'm So-So* when he reveals, "I have private ties to God. I ask Him for things, like *jasnosc*. Sometimes He grants them, sometimes He doesn't." (The subtitles say "clear intellectual overview," but the Polish word *jasnosc* is closer to illumination or lucidity.) Perhaps this belief can be linked to the two appearances of the "angel" in *2:* the young man is present when slides reveal the patient's "progression"; and he is in the background of the unresponsive husband's hospital room when Dorota tells him she loves him. Both moments could be seen as turning points in the patient's movement back to life.

The doctor's remark, "We don't treat X rays but people," invokes the very commandment to which *2* could be connected—but which is absent from the literal list that was formulated after filming: "Thou shalt not make unto thee any graven image."

Decalogue, 3

Domestic drama continues to be the focus for Kieslowski in both *3* and *4.* The third episode takes place on Christmas Eve, with Janusz (Daniel Olbrychski) coming home dressed up as Santa Claus. He takes his wife and children to Midnight Mass, where he glimpses his former lover, Eva (Maria Pakulnis). She later rings his bell, upset that her husband Edward has disappeared; Janusz tells his wife someone has stolen his taxi and reluctantly spends the night driving around with Eva. By morning, she confesses that Edward left her three years ago—precisely after finding her in bed with Janusz—and that she made a bet with herself: if Janusz spent the night with her, in any form, she would not kill herself. He returns to his wife, who suspected all along that he was with Eva.

Whereas the screenplay introduces Eva only in church, the film crosscuts her presence throughout the beginning. We see her driving a red car into the neighborhood and spying on Janusz's family. She then visits her aged aunt in a senior center: Eva's tender treatment of what might be her only living relative

Janusz and Eva in *Decalogue, 3*

creates sympathy. Moreover, the aunt speaks to her as if she were still a child—did she do her homework?—suggesting that she might have raised Eva. (Was Eva an orphan like the protagonists of *Camera Buff* and *Blind Chance*?) This sympathetic moment offsets the depiction of a woman who turns out to be a manipulative liar. (If she lies to Janusz about not having attended Midnight Mass, he also lies to his wife about their taxi being missing.)

Even before Eva suggests—via a pill falling from her pocket—that she would have committed suicide if Janusz had not remained with her till morning, the idea of death is invoked by close-ups of a rusty razor. When Janusz is about to enter her apartment, she hastily takes out and displays possessions of Edward: among these are a razor and brush, which she dips in water. Janusz sees the razor, opens it, tries the blade on his hand and notes how blunt it is. He even asks Eva if Edward has grown a beard. She then closes the bathroom door and tries the razor blade against her hand. Although it elicits no blood, self-destruction is invoked. (Ironically, when she shows him a photo of Edward at the end, he does sport a beard!)

Kieslowski tells this story through expressive camera work, especially with light and glass. The first shot is of blurred lights that come into focus when a drunk appears. ("Where is my home?" he moans, suggesting the desolation found in previous sections of *The Decalogue*.) Light itself is foregrounded here, as is the camera's power to clarify sight. Later, a police car following Janusz's "stolen" taxi is presented with a close-up of flashing blue light. Kieslowski then reveals the partiality of the image, as red and white lights join the blue. The light is especially striking at the train station in the morning, where Eva confesses to her ruse: only their eyes are fully lit, calling attention to the new honesty between them. When they finally part, the headlights of their cars do the talking: each affectionately emits two short flares at the other.

As in other segments of *The Decalogue*, close-ups—combined with wider shots that contain variations of lighting—tend to isolate characters. Even when they share the frame in physical proximity, each is lit differently: if one is in shadow and the other in light, the formal separation expresses an emotional state. Kieslowski's choice of camera angle adds layers to the meaning of many shots. For example, our introduction to Janusz's family is mediated by Krzysztof, the father of Pavel from *1*, who is leaving the building as "Santa Claus" enters. The camera pans from his point of view to Janusz's first-floor window: we thus see the celebrating family through the eyes of a man who has lost his own.

Similarly, when Eva visits her aunt, the camera remains on a lamp and its reflection in the window. As Eva leaves, the camera moves toward the window through which we see her drive off—perhaps the point of view of the aunt who will remain alone. There is little natural light in this nocturnal film, and the omnipresent glass—as in Douglas Sirk's motion pictures—conveys separation.

Vincent Amiel perceptively notes the connections between *3* and *My Night at Maud's*: "As with Rohmer, Kieslowski's hero notices a young woman at Midnight Mass and, as with Rohmer, he is led into a trap by an older woman. But here the two women are one, and the image of the younger woman is three years too late."[16] This comparison is especially apt given the larger connections between *The Decalogue* and Rohmer's cinematic series, *Six Moral Tales*. Both filmmakers deal with chance, faith, and self-delusion, allowing adult characters to speak their minds—and inviting adult viewers to reflect upon issues. Kieslowski acknowledged in 1989, "Unfortunately I don't know all of Rohmer's films, but I liked very much the ones I saw. They had a strong influence on me, especially 'Claire's Knee.' But I wasn't aware [until recently] that he adopted this 'series' approach twice."[17]

Of the two filmmakers, Kieslowski goes further in evoking the socio-political framework that informs his characters. For example, the nocturnal journey of Eva and Janusz includes depressing visits not only to the morgue but to a prison-like

Decalogue, 3

"drying-out centre" (p. 76) where drunks are cruelly hosed down. On this holy night in Poland, compassion seems to be in short supply.

Decalogue, 4

If parts *2* and *3* of *The Decalogue* explore the difficult aftermath of adulterous relationships, the fourth segment returns to the far more troubling dramatic terrain of *1,* namely, the bond of a father and child. Engaging but disturbing, *4*—a somewhat ironic twist on the commandment "Honor thy father and mother"—deals with incestuous desire. Anka (Adrianna Biedrzynska), a twenty-year-old acting student, lives happily with her widowed father Michal (Janusz Gajos). She is intrigued by an envelope in his drawer that says, "To be opened only after my death." Succumbing to temptation, she opens the envelope when he is away and finds inside it a sealed letter from her mother (who died shortly after her birth). Anka confronts Michal with the knowledge that he is not her real father—thereby liberating her incestuous feelings for him. Although he acknowledges his own troubled romantic stirrings, Michal refuses to act upon them. Anka finally confesses that she did not open her mother's envelope: she wrote the letter—a script of possible wish fulfillment—as if she were her mother. Anka burns the original, with Michal's blessing, as they attempt to return to domestic normalcy.

With a slight nod to religious context, if *3* takes place on Christmas Eve, *4* begins on Easter Monday. This not only leads to the playful scene of Anka and Michal throwing water on each other (a Polish custom, according to the screenplay) but introduces the theme of transformation that is central to Easter. Anka is indeed an actress—her very profession depends on transformation—and she has in a sense been "acting" the role of daughter (despite a suspicion that biological history might allow for a change of roles).

Whereas the script shows her performing a scene from *The Glass Menagerie* in acting class, the film changes the text to *Romeo and Juliet*—the latter perhaps more appropriate to a film about interdiction to romance. And, as Françoise Audé points out, "Anka has trouble expressing love in acting class exercises. When her professor—a man of the same generation as her father—takes her partner's place, she succeeds: she becomes a lover."[18] Many of the other changes from screenplay to final version foreground Michal's conflicted feelings. For example, Kieslowski added a scene in which the father eavesdrops on Anka's phone conversation when she tells her boyfriend that she finally got her period. After she claims to have read the letter, she asks her father, "What should I call you?" "Daddy," he replies in the script. However, "I don't know," is the response in the film. But if the screenplay had Michal finally leaving to stay with a friend, he is merely going out to get milk before the movie ends. In the original ending of Kieslowski and Piesiewicz, Michal tells Anka a story about a man who was able to race through traffic on his bicycle because he didn't see well; once he put on glasses, he could no longer move. The film replaces this verbal presentation with a visual one: instead of a story, we see an old photo above Anka's bed of her mother accompanied by two men (one of whom might be her father).

The story about glasses would have been more relevant, however, to the pattern of imagery developed throughout *4*. Anka goes to an eye doctor for glasses; when asked to read let-

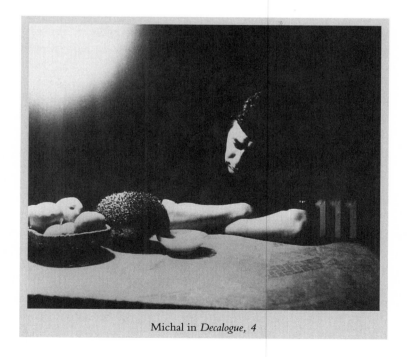

Michal in *Decalogue, 4*

ters on a board, she pronounces, significantly enough, F . . . A . . . T . . . H . . . E . . . R. When Michal returns home after Anka's confrontation, we see him seated through a glass door. At first, it is not clear whether the camera is slowly turning, or the door. A shadow passes before his face. He slams the moving door shut and it breaks. We then see Michal through the shattered area, as if in a split screen. Subsequently, he plays with small vodka glasses. For those who might recall Kieslowski's earlier female characters with shattered glass at their feet, it is a surprise when he does not break them: Michal might be capable of greater control than Urszula or Dorota. (Moreover, even a pair of scissors that Anka takes from the house to open the forbidden letter in the woods look like glasses.)

She buries these scissors after our familiar "angel" passes by. He is carrying a gondola, and when he walks by Anka holding the letter, his gaze prevents her from opening it. The fact that he carries a boat provides two symbolic layers: holding it up, his body suggests a cross shape—appropriate to the Easter season—and the boat connects to the water in the Winston cigarette poster above Anka's bed.

The "angel" is also present when she tells Michal she lied about reading her mother's letter. If the "angel" is thus linked to truth, it is worth noting that Anka is not the only one who lies in *4:* Michal claims that a draft broke the glass door. By the end, Anka has cleared the air, setting the stage for the resumption of father–daughter roles. From the water of the opening image, we have moved to the purging fire of the burning letter, and from blurred sight to the clarity permitted by glasses.

The emphasis on glass and the gaze invokes the Oedipus tale, which ends in blindness. Kieslowski might be offering a contemporary reversal: instead of the unwitting child sleeping with a parent—and then being destroyed by the discovery—here the child goes on a quest to deny the parental bond precisely in order to sleep with the parent. This, of course, begs the question of whether paternity is purely a question of biology. Isn't the man who raised Anka from birth her "real" father, no matter where the sperm originated? Michal's perception that "in films children are always trying to find their real fathers" (p. 101) is certainly true, but Anka seems more interested in finding her "real lover." The added irony is that her ultimate way of truly honoring the father is to disobey the mother—by destroying her precious letter.

Decalogue, 5

Episode 5 can be seen as a detour from the emotional terrain of the first four segments of *The Decalogue*. After all, *1* and *4* deal with a father–child relationship, whereas *2* and *3* focus on the aftermath of adultery. *Decalogue, 5*—and its longer version, *A Short Film about Killing*—is physically removed from the apartment complex and dramatically far from the domestic frame in which women play a central role. It tells the more brutal story of a disaffected young man, Jacek (Miroslaw Baka), who murders a taxi driver (Jan Tesarz) living in the complex and is then defended by an idealistic lawyer, Piotr (Krzysztof Globisz). Jacek is sentenced and finally executed by the state.

The first four parts of *The Decalogue* offer character motivation that invites sympathy for protagonists. *Decalogue, 5,* how-

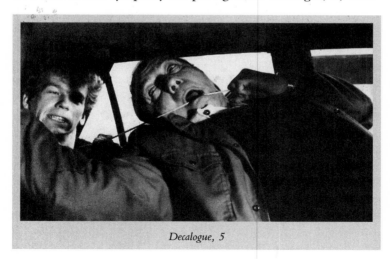

Decalogue, 5

ever, is a more difficult cinematic experience because it provides almost no background for either the victim or the murderer, thereby denying viewer identification. Indeed, the first thing we see the driver do is play a nasty joke on Dorota and her husband from *Decalogue, 2*[19]: needing a ride on this cold day, they wait for him to finish washing his taxi, but he zips off without them. And if emotion tends to be suppressed in *1* through *4,* here the focus is on violent release. Moreover, the murder is presented in horrifying detail and length (approximately seven minutes), stretching audience tolerance: it is not meant to be easily digested.

For no apparent reason, Jacek instructs the driver to take a deserted road, then suddenly places around his neck the rope he has been winding in his hands. The strangling is not enough to kill the struggling driver, so Jacek then beats him and finally bashes his head in with a rock. Intercut with these actions is a speeding train (perhaps symbolic of implacable fate, as in Emile Zola's *La Bête Humaine*), whose whistle drowns out the sound of the taxi's horn that might have alerted a passerby to the crime. We also see a horse turning its head to the sound of the horn. The enigmatic animal is no more able to stop what is happening than the "angel," who appears before the murder: crossing Jacek's path, he seems to be shaking his head, as if to warn the young man not to fulfill his plans.

The "angel" is seen again before the execution, supporting the visual "rhyme" of the two murder sequences. Even if the Biblical injunction of "an eye for an eye" seems to justify the death of Jacek, the graphic authenticity of the execution is as difficult to watch as the first killing. Kieslowski precedes the scene with the preparations for sanctioned murder: a man checks to make sure the gallows are working. Significantly enough, he begins by opening a curtain in the room. This not only conveys a sense of spectacle—the execution is as much for society's spectators as for the accused—but of malfunction: the curtain is stuck.

Decalogue, 5 does not merely mirror these two murders. A third killing is invoked when Jacek tells Piotr at the end about the accidental death of his younger sister Marysia five years earlier: she was run over by a drunk on a tractor—another "driver." His sole request is to be buried in the family grave, where there were three plots—and now only one remains. (His continued mourning for Marysia explains why Jacek has been drawn to little girls or their images earlier in the film.)

As in *Blind Chance,* Kieslowski uses a triadic structure, in which three seemingly unconnected characters will intersect. The introduction juxtaposes the three men: we hear Piotr's voice-over musings on the legal system—as he is about to undergo the examination that will render him a lawyer—before we see him framed in a mirror; the driver is presented as glass reflects the apartment complex; Jacek is introduced in the street, reflected in a window as well. The glass image recurs throughout the film, notably in the movie theater where Jacek is told by a bored female cashier that the film isn't being shown; the windshield through which we see the taxi driver; the photo shop window through which Jacek stares at pictures of little girls; and the café where Jacek has a snack and flings his coffee spoon against the window. As in Kieslowski's previous work, glass serves to self-consciously foreground the act of looking.

Mirrors abound in *5* as well, such as the taxi's rear-view mirror in which Jacek is reflected and the side mirror in which he is briefly framed during the murder sequence. "There are many reflections in my film," Kieslowski said in *Télérama,* "through windows, through doors . . . because this horrible story reflects the world. And for the reflection to be true, it has to be disgusting."[20] These reflections connect to the film's structural mirroring of murders—that of the driver by Jacek, and of Jacek by the state. (In 1987, Poland was enforcing capital punishment.) This is appropriate to a film that questions sight and its moral consequences: during the first murder sequence, what can a viewer stand to watch? And in terms of the final execution, what can a member of civilized society bear to see?

Kieslowski's internal frames also separate characters, heightening their isolation. Piotr, for example, is seen from the beginning in solitary shots. Whereas the screenplay shows his fiancée, *5* merely has him call her from the courthouse. And in one of the film's most striking visual compositions, his visit to Jacek after the trial is presented in terms of split-screen technique. When he enters, the frame is divided vertically, and each character is lit by his own window in the background. When they sit down, Kieslowski cuts back and forth from a close-up of Jacek to one of Piotr, their faces partially lit from the windows.

These compositions relate to the overriding visual strategy of *5,* which stresses alienation. Warsaw seems like a despairing place: around Jacek, boys chase and fight each other while an old woman feeding pigeons yells at him. In the square, Jacek in the foreground seems completely removed from people in the background of the shot. At one point, he looks at a taxi stand through a frame created by his arm and elbow; when he returns the armpit to his body, the screen goes to black. And toward the end of the murder scene, it is through the frame of the open taxi door that we see Jacek dragging the driver's body to the river.

The alienation extends to the internal landscape of a character like Jacek. Whereas the screenplay (and longer film version) suggests a possible reason for his violent act, *5* deletes it. Piesiewicz and Kieslowski included the character of Beata, with whom the driver flirts before he leaves the complex. She turns out to be a surprising link between him and Jacek when the young man drives the victim's taxi back to the apartment building. He rings for Beata, who comes down and, with growing horror, recognizes the cab. "You always said you wanted to go away," Jacek tells her. "Now we can go wherever you like. I can leave the hostel now—and you can leave your mum's" (pp. 137–8).

Because there is no such scene in *5,* the driver's murder is closer to what André Gide explored in his novel *Les Caves du Vatican* and Albert Camus in *L'Etranger*: Like an existentialist hero, Jacek commits *l'acte gratuit*—the gratuitous or arbitrary

Decalogue, 5

act. His victim seems chosen at random. Eric Derobert has written persuasively that

> the future assassin is a man perpetually waiting and almost
> always disappointed, as with the movie for which he arrives
> too late. . . . The taxi driver, on the other hand, never stops
> disappointing the people waiting for him. By chance these
> two characters come together because the young man
> reaches the taxi station a second before two other people. At
> this point, the attitude of the two protagonists is inverted for
> the first time. . . . [They are] unified by the complementary
> quality of repeated contempt and accumulated rejection.[21]

Kieslowski replaces Jacek's connection to the driver via Beata with
a deeper tie to Piotr. Indeed, many of the changes from the script
heighten the lawyer's importance. He opens and closes the film,
beginning with a voice-over that stresses the machinery of the state
system rather than the soon-to-be killer and victim. His presence
at the end—sitting alone in a car and yelling, "I abhor nature"—
provides a dark rhyme to Jacek seated in the taxi after the murder.

During Piotr's examination, he is a small figure in the background while a glass of tea dominates the frame in the foreground; later, tea is precisely what Jacek requests and cannot obtain in the café. If Marysia—the child closest to Jacek—has died, the lawyer is congratulated before the execution for the birth of his son. And Piotr's voice is often a sound bridge, accompanying images of Jacek. His ruminations illustrate a beautifully troubling comment made by Josef Tischner at the 1997 Paris colloquium:

> "The Decalogue" is a film about the memory of "paradise lost"—a time when the Ten Commandments still had meaning because a human being felt capable of choosing between good and evil. . . . People will kill each other, and in this killing feel innocent; they won't be able to love—nor feel responsible for that—but it will hurt. Why? Not because they have a bad conscience, but because they remember that maybe once there was a time when things were different.

Kieslowski also added to *5* a few scenes that convey Jacek's violence, foreshadowing the punishment (when he enters the movie theater, he is framed behind bars) as well as the crime. Jacek pushes a rock from a bridge onto a crowded highway, and we hear the sound of an accident. In a urinal, he throws down a man who smiles at him. Even a detail like Jacek spitting into his coffee cup before he leaves the café adds to the portrait of an anti-social and dangerous loner. And whereas a Hollywood film probably would have centered on a courtroom scene in which Jacek's troubled adolescence might inspire sympathy, the total deletion of a trial removes the possibility of justification from his crime. As Kieslowski put it, "I wasn't interested in the trial. We know what the lawyers could say, and the sentence. What interested me most is that which exists behind the scenes of a human being's soul, behind the scenes of the murder."[22]

The cinematic details are even more painful to behold in *A Short Film about Killing*. Jacek is introduced in the context of a dead rat in green water—prefiguring his dragging the cabdriver to the river—and a cat hanging: the rope prepares for the one he latches onto the driver's neck, as well as his own noose at the end. The green water is later invoked by the sickly fluorescent light at his execution. In this version, Jacek's death is followed by a shot of his excrement oozing into the pan below the body. Kieslowski credited his cinematographer Slawomir Idziak with the idea of deliberate visual unattractiveness: "I sense that the world around me is becoming more and more ugly. . . . I wanted to dirty this world. . . . We used green filters that give this strange effect, allowing us to mask all that isn't essential to the image."[23] Although *A Short Film about Killing* may be stomach churning, it won not only the Jury Prize at the 1988 Cannes Film Festival but the "Felix"—the first European Film Award.

Decalogue, 6

Episode *6* and the expanded theatrical version, *A Short Film about Love,*[24] constitute the most lyrical portion of *The Decalogue*. Although the film—which some critics have connected to "Thou shalt not commit adultery"—can be considered an exploration of voyeurism, Zbigniew Preisner's score renders *6* a love story as well. His tender melodies accompany Tomek (Olaf Lubaszenko), a timid postal worker, and—as his name suggests—"a Peeping Tom." He is obsessed with Magda (Grazyna Szapolowska), a free-wheeling artist who lives across the courtyard. Every night, his alarm clock rings at 8:30, her time of arrival home: this is when Tomek "wakes up," truly alive only when watching her. In addition, he places phony money orders in her mailbox to draw her to the post office.

Tomek finally confesses his love to Magda, who agrees to go out with him. They return to her apartment, where she leads his trembling hand up her naked thighs. He climaxes immediately, and she dismisses him with a curt, "That's all it comes down to, Love. Now go to the bathroom and clean yourself up." In his own bathroom, Tomek slits his wrists, while Magda—unaware of the suicide attempt—is overcome by guilt simply for treating him unkindly. Tomek is nineteen—the same age as Jacek in *A Short Film about Killing*—and, like the disaffected murderer, a loner. But this gentle protagonist is saved by the maternal presence of his landlady (Stefania Iwinska), the mother of his friend who is abroad.

While he recovers in the hospital, Magda realizes her deeper feelings for him and tries unsuccessfully to visit Tomek. The landlady, having spied on the erotic moment between them through her boarder's telescope, will not facilitate Magda's attempt. When Magda finally sees Tomek at the post office in the last scene, he says, "I no longer spy on you," as if he had gotten over Magda.

The opening of *6* goes further than previous segments of *The Decalogue* in establishing glass as a central motif and symbol: it separates people at the same time that it allows for the penetration of sight. At Tomek's post office window, Magda is reflected on the glass through which we see the young man. In the next scene, glass shatters when Tomek breaks into the place from which he steals a telephoto lens. Magda is simultaneously seen through her glass window; since our voyeur is not yet home, it is indeed Kieslowski's camera that spies on her, taking its cue from the binoculars positioned at Tomek's window.

They are replaced by the stolen lens, which enables Tomek to zoom in for close-ups. But when he later sees Magda welcoming a lover—who places his hands inside her flimsy panties—Tomek looks away, implying that love (rather than lust) inspires his gaze. And when a new man (who presumably came to appraise her tapestries) embarks on a sexual embrace, Tomek graduates from mere voyeurism to active "directing": he calls the gas company to report a phony leak in Magda's apartment, thereby interrupting their lovemaking as the gas investigators knock on her door. (The connection between the Peeping Tom and the director is strengthened by the fact that Olaf Lubaszenko is the assistant director of *The Decalogue*.)

A Short Film about Love is far richer than *6* in its elaboration of romance and the complex relationship between viewer and object. With completely different openings and endings (both of which have little in common with the screenplay), the longer version suggests a deeper exchange between Tomek and Magda. Each is introduced in solitude: he is peering across the courtyard behind binoculars; she plays solitaire. Each eats alone, accompanied by Preisner's yearning melody. But Magda is soon visited by a lover, and Tomek's landlady invites him to watch *Miss Polonia* on TV with her. Tomek has no desire to see women parading—deliberately posing—in a sanctioned frame when he can spy on his unwitting object. He kisses his landlady's hand and returns to his room.

The imagery of hands is central to *A Short Film about Love*. During the opening credit sequence, a hand tries to touch a bandaged hand but is stopped by another hand. The camera pans to the sleeping Tomek, confirming that a third party has prevented the caress of his bandaged hand. In a matter of seconds, Kieslowski manages to introduce three of the crucial elements in *A Short Film about Love*—a yearning for contact, interdiction, and a suicide attempt. In retrospect, this is Magda reaching for Tomek, denied by the landlady. We can interpret the scene as a flash-forward, or as a structural detail that renders the entire film a flashback; in the latter reading, the circular structure suggests a pessimistic inescapability rather than the possibility of forward progression.

The introduction of hands—as in the credit sequence of François Truffaut's *The Soft Skin*—prepares for their importance throughout the film. When they first go out, Magda holds her pendulum device over Tomek's hand and, satisfied with its circular motion, shows him how to stroke her hand. This contact is more satisfying than the close-ups of Tomek's fingers curled around the telescope while gazing. The vulnerability of hands is suggested when he plays a knife game (seen in Roman Polanski's *Knife in the Water*): with his fingers spread out, he taps the sharp point quickly between them—until he cuts himself. (His bandaged hand foreshadows the suicide attempt—his slit wrists in close-up—which will later be patched up.) At the same time, as Magda cries alone in her apartment and spills a bottle of milk on the table, her finger moves helplessly in the white puddle. The characters are indeed connected by the juxtaposition of his bloody finger and hers in the soothing milk.

Milk is another recurring image in *6* and *A Short Film about Love*. In order to see Magda up close, Tomek becomes a milk deliveryman for the apartment complex, replacing her empty bottles with fresh ones. Milk symbolizes not only Tomek's innocence but the maternal fluid that was denied him: as we learn from his conversation with the landlady, his mother abandoned him, and he was raised in an orphanage. The spilled milk on Magda's table can be likened to Tomek's wasted semen during his sole visit to her apartment. (In *Decalogue, 6* only, milk is spilled again when she abruptly opens her door while Tomek is making the delivery.)

The white of the milk is also part of the deliberate white-red–blue color scheme that permeates *The Decalogue* as well as Kieslowski's subsequent *Three Colors* trilogy. A red tone seems to surround Magda, from the tapestries she makes to her very red phone. Tomek, on the other hand, wears blue, from the light shade of his post office uniform to the dark blue turtleneck during milk delivery. Indeed, when Magda asks him during this scene what he wants from her, they are framed by the hallway window: the white of the window square is surrounded by a red background.

Red is the color of the cloth he keeps over his telescope. It is also, of course, the color of blood, seen when Tomek cuts his finger and later when his slit wrists—in a basin of white water—emit red spurts. But blood is in actuality blue: only when combined with oxygen (outside the skin) does it becomes red. Even the circular dots on the glass door of the building—seen when Magda asks the old mailman what happened to Tomek—are red: they are perhaps a warning to birds, to keep them from flying into the illusion of open space.

On Magda's window is a similar circular reflector, prominent in almost every shot of her apartment. Such circular images tie the film and its characters together. For example, the reflector connects Magda to the cylindrical telescope through which Tomek watches her—notably in the striking early close-up of his eye poised behind the lens. Kieslowski also includes the hole in Tomek's post office window; the flashlight's circular beam that enables him to find and steal the telescope; Tomek's alarm clock—which alerts him at 8:30 nightly that it's time to watch Magda's entrance—juxtaposed with her grandfather clock, containing circular parts hanging beneath the face; the hole he jubilantly punches in the wall after his gas company ruse succeeds; a paperweight she offers him; and the round basin in which he slits his wrists.

This imagery coexists with a deeper circularity, namely how the last scene of *A Short Film about Love* brings Magda full circle to Tomek's telescope. When she looks through it into her own apartment, she sees what appears to be a flashback: Magda comes home alone, spills the bottle of milk on the table, and cries—as if the telescope were a camera that had recorded that night. But this grows into an imagined scene of Tomek entering her apartment and comforting Magda. Since this scene is presented in slow motion, she is essentially staging it like a wish fulfillment. The film ends with Magda closing her eyes, unable to continue as either voyeur or object. (Kieslowski invented this conclusion after the actress begged him for a happier ending than the script allowed.)

That Tomek and Magda have exchanged roles is heightened by the music: Preisner's first melody—in which the notes descend before rising again—tends to accompany Magda; Tomek is often seen as we hear a cello solo whose notes rise before they descend again. Later, the cello accompanies Magda when she realizes her deeper feelings for the now-absent Tomek: holding her own opera glasses up to the window, she tries in vain to attract his gaze. His guilt for spying on her (as well as stealing the telescope) is replaced by her guilt for treating him cruelly.

Whereas Tomek may be the central "Peeping Tom" in this film, Kieslowski extends voyeurism to all the major characters, suggesting how easily one can take the place of the other.

Tomek has assumed the role of his friend Marcin, who left him not only his room but his binoculars (with which Marcin was already watching Magda). When Tomek finally goes to her apartment, his landlady—Marcin's mother—looks anxiously at them through his telescope. She then allows Magda to peer through Tomek's "extended eye" into Magda's own apartment, leading to the haunting scene of their imagined reunion.

Even the "angel"—the pure gaze of the entire *Decalogue*—returns at crucial instances in *6:* when Magda has agreed to go out with Tomek, he smiles while observing Tomek excitedly pulling his milk truck in a triumphant circle. But after she has dismissed him, the "angel" passes the humiliated Tomek rushing back across the courtyard. His very presence suggests that Kieslowski's voyeurism here is quite different from that of Hitchcock, especially in films like *Psycho* and *Rear Window*. The Master of Suspense dwelled on guilt, implicitly punishing both characters and viewers who waited for (or willed) violence to erupt. In Kieslowski's hands, the gaze can be sympathetic rather than merely sexual, protective rather than prurient. After all, the

Magda and Tomek in *Decalogue, 6*

landlady presumably finds Tomek before his suicide succeeds precisely because she watched how he fled Magda's place.

Like the "angel," we are silent witnesses to the futile efforts of Tomek and Magda. Even the constant diegetic sounds of the courtyard contribute to an aural voyeurism that is part of modern urban life. For example, once Magda is aware that Tomek is spying, she tauntingly moves her bed closer to the window, keeps the light on when her bearded lover arrives, and tells him they are being watched; he runs angrily into the courtyard. Although the film does not subtitle his cry of "Postman"— which would alert the landlady, among others, to the fact that Tomek is the "coward" being yelled for—we realize that neighbors have to hear the fight. If *A Short Film about Love* succeeds in making us identify with Magda looking through the telescope in the last scene, we too are ultimately able to see more than what is perceptually visible, able to feel both regret and hope. Whereas *5* and *A Short Film about Killing* distance the viewer from the characters, *6* and *A Short Film about Love* invite us to vicariously experience a gaze filled with longing.

What makes *A Short Film about Love* plausible as a love story is that Tomek is more active here than in *6*. We see more of him stealing the telescope (whereas he buys it in the script), as well as volunteering for milk delivery. We also see Tomek mustering the courage to ask Magda out: he goes up to the roof and, reminiscent of Krzysztof at the end of *1*, places ice on his ears. After tasting the ice, he gets the idea to invite her for ice cream. Moreover, the exchange of roles is enhanced: with the new last scene, Magda is the object-turned-subject, taking Tomek's place at the telescope.

Indeed, many of the deletions from the screenplay to the final film render Tomek less awkward. In the script, after seeing Magda's lover make a furtive phone call when she is in the bathroom, he runs out to the parking lot and puts darts in the man's tires. He is also seen borrowing Marcin's ill-fitting suit for the date and, in the café with Magda, asking the waitress the price of a glass of wine. In the film, he does not look or sound as childish.

The film version makes it more believable that Magda would say the following lines—which, significantly enough, were added to the screenplay—when they leave the café: "If we catch that bus, you'll come up to my place. OK?" The bus begins to leave while they run. But it stops again, they board, and the next shot reveals Tomek in Magda's apartment. As in Kieslowski's previous films, one must wonder whether chance or fate is responsible for their sexual interchange, albeit aborted; or did the bus driver stop precisely because he saw them running so determinedly toward him?

The fact that Magda brazenly accepts Tomek's peeping (after all, she could have bought curtains!) calls to mind *Monsieur Hire,* Patrice Leconte's 1989 drama starring Michel Blanc as a voyeur obsessed with a young woman played by Sandrine Bonnaire. But if this French psychological mystery (adapted from Simenon) does indeed depict the woman seducing the man who has been spying on her, it turns out to be part of a plot to protect her boyfriend, a murderer. Monsieur Hire, realizing she has betrayed him, finally jumps from the very window that allowed him to gaze at her. Leconte's film is thus closer than *A Short Film about Love* to the Hitchcockian notion of how easily the voyeur can become the victim.

Kieslowski's film seems to have more in common with Krzysztof Zanussi's *Inventory,* made around the same time. Again, there are three central characters: Tomas, an innocent young student, his decent mother (Maja Komorowska), and the older woman, Julia (Krystyna Janda), a self-destructive former newspaper censor. He brings Julia home, where she creates tension. They become lovers, despite his mother's justifiable wariness. At the end, he is reconciled with his mother—holding hands over the table—and then he visits Julia at a psychiatric home, taking her hands through the bars. Zanussi seems to suggest that Tomas's faith in Julia will redeem her. Given that these films were made in the late 1980s, Magda and Julia might lend themselves to a political interpretation. If father figures are absent—a rejection of the paternal state?—perhaps Magda and Julia symbolize a corrupt Poland that is capable of redemption through innocent faith and love.

Decalogue, 7

There is a continuity between the endings of 6 and 7 where an older woman stops a younger one (who has "sinned") from going through with her plan. Women are indeed depicted as the stronger sex in both segments: if the dramatic focus of *1* is between father and son, and that of *4* between father and daughter, 7 addresses the mother–daughter connection. Loosely based on the commandment "Thou shalt not steal," this episode explores theft on a variety of levels. Majka (Maja Barelkowska) kidnaps her six-year-old sister Ania, who is in reality her daughter. When Majka's mother Eva (Anna Polony) discovered the teenaged Majka's pregnancy six years earlier, they agreed—to avoid a scandal—that Eva would be the mother. The sullen Majka can no longer accept the situation: after being expelled from school, she takes Ania to see Wojtek (Boguslaw Linda), the child's biological father. He has not seen Majka in years and is hardly comfortable with their visit. A loner too, Wojtek has left school and makes teddy bears in his one large room.

The distraught Eva and her husband Stefan (Wladyslaw Kowalski) search for Ania; when Majka calls, they are initially relieved but then stunned to hear their daughter demanding her rights of motherhood. Although Wojtek reluctantly lets them stay in his shack, Majka escapes with Ania. They are finally discovered at the train station, where Ania hugs Eva as "Mama," and Majka jumps onto a departing train alone.

Decalogue, 7 is a film of frustration, beginning with the off-screen scream of a child in the opening credits. Because there is no visible source for the sound—and it is not until four scenes later that we see the child comforted—tension accumulates. Whereas the screenplay shows Ania crying, then hearing Eva's lullaby and relaxing, Kieslowski postpones the release: his exploratory camera tilts down the outside of the apartment

Eva and Ania in *Decalogue, 7*

building; then we see Majka telling a secretary she won't appeal to stay in school; Stefan is working with wood while the scream continues; Majka arranges for her passport; finally, she tries in vain to comfort the screaming girl but must yield to Eva, the only one who knows how to calm Ania. The frustration felt by the audience throughout the opening sequence prepares us for that of Majka, waiting to flee the false domestic arrangement with her daughter.

But as in Kieslowski's other films, the image of Majka behind the glass of the passport office—rhymed at the end by her face behind the train window—suggests separation. The first close-up of hands are those on her shoulder as she tries to calm the screaming Ania. But instead of providing comfort, the hand turns out to be that of her mother pushing Majka aside so that Eva can quiet the child. Majka's essential loneliness prevails, despite a noteworthy change from the screenplay in which Wojtek calms the screaming Ania: in the film, Majka is the one who succeeds in soothing her. But Kieslowski also deletes a scene that anchors Majka in an affectionate relationship: the script shows her visiting her former dance teacher in order to sneak into the area where Ania is watching a puppet show; the teacher tells her, "You're one of the best students I ever taught! . . . such a happy, smiling girl." In the film, Majka gets backstage by distracting a female caretaker with a ball that falls down the stairs.

Images of loneliness abound in 7. For example, Kieslowski added two scenes of Ania on a merry-go-round: during the first, Majka spies on her from behind shrubs; during the second, after they have escaped, Ania rides a deserted merry-go-round. The forlorn carousel invokes lost childhood, just as Wojtek's

Ania and Majka in *Decalogue,* 7

menagerie of teddy bears are lifeless without children. It is Eva who feels abandonment acutely: "I've lost my child," she wails after the children leave the puppet show, but no one responds. And whereas the "angel" is at least a sympathetic presence in other parts of *The Decalogue,* he is not even recognizable in 7. The script presents him on crutches at the train station, but Kieslowski acknowledged that shooting problems rendered the footage unusable.

In the screenplay, Eva's husband Stefan seems more integral to the story, perhaps because he makes organ whistles (juxtaposed with a scream, a moan, and a lullaby). But in the film, he works only with wood in his room and seems less capable of creating something. Kieslowski also deletes his political background: in the script only, he is a lapsed Communist Party member who disappointed his colleagues during martial law. The film presents him as a resigned background figure, someone who was aware of Eva's lack of love for Majka and excessive affection for Ania. He says that Eva screamed when she saw Majka six months pregnant. Since the cause of Ania's loud nightmares is never dealt with, perhaps it is symbolically related to the scream of Eva while Ania was in Majka's womb.

Wojtek observes that Ania's scream is for the future. In this sense, the opening sound of 7 is premonitory, suggesting that Ania knows something is amiss. While it is true that, as Majka tells Eva, "You stole my daughter," this is not the only theft revealed in the film. Eva was perhaps overly eager to be Ania's mother because she could not have more children—"robbed" of the chance to procreate further. One could also say that Wojtek stole Majka's childhood, but then again, Eva robbed him of the chance to be a father. "I've lost my child," she cries after the puppet show, foreshadowing the loss of both daughters. Perhaps Majka thinks Ania stole Eva's love from her? And, as she asks, "Can you steal something that belongs to you?" Because Eva won't tell Majka all she knows about Wojtek—who was a teacher in the school where Eva was headmistress and Majka a student—there is also the possibility that Wojtek had an affair with Eva. "You haven't had much luck with our family, have you?" Eva asks Wojtek as they search for the girls.

The film's imagery and color scheme connect 7 to Kieslowski's other work. He adds shots of peaceful blue water during the search: when Ania throws a twig, the camera follows the rushing stream that takes it. Given the director's predilection for blue-white-red patterns, it is noteworthy that Ania wears a red sweater and white blouse, and that Wojtek is introduced hanging white sheets before being seen by his red phone. *Decalogue, 7* ends with Majka jumping onto a train; as in *Blind Chance,* it is less suggestive of freedom than of a fixed course. Like that of Witek in the previous film, Majka's destiny seems rooted not in biology but in the accumulated actions that reveal character. *Decalogue, 7* is also rooted in one of Piesiewicz's legal cases: he said in an interview,

> In reality, the father of the little girl was also the grandfather. It was an incest story . . . the grandmother had agreed to pass as the mother in the eyes of the neighbors. When I knew the young woman, she was 17. In my opinion, 3 years later she would logically be led to kidnap her own child.[25]

Decalogue, 8

The credit sequence of *8*—which does not exist in the script—is continuous with 7: as they are walking, an adult takes a child's hand in close-up. This image of trust will turn out to be a flashback to World War II, a fragment that is subject to question as the film progresses. The focus, as in the preceding episode, is on the relationship between two women: the older one is Zofia (Maria Koscialkowska), a respected professor of philosophy, and the younger is Elzbieta (Teresa Marczewska), visiting Warsaw from New York. It will turn out that they met briefly more than forty years earlier. In Zofia's class—where students propose examples of "ethical hell"—Elzbieta tells a true story that

Elzbieta *(top)* and Zofia *(bottom)* in *Decalogue, 8*

seems to discomfort the professor: in 1943, a six-year-old Jewish girl is brought to hide in a couple's Warsaw apartment. The
woman who was supposed to protect the girl tells her that they
have to withdraw the offer because their religion forbids the
bearing of false witness (lying to authorities). The Jewish girl,
unable to understand, must leave.

After a brief class discussion of motives and possible justification, the professor ends the session. From the looks on their
faces, we see that each of the two women now knows that the
story refers to her own past: Zofia, the one who turned away
the girl, is relieved to learn that—despite her inability to help in
1943—the child survived. And Elzbieta realizes that Zofia, who
was working with the underground resistance, had good reasons for the seemingly inexplicable abandonment when the
professor tells Elzbieta, "We had received information that
the people who were due to hide the girl were agents of the
Gestapo, and that through her . . . they would eventually have
been led to us." Zofia adds that the information about these
people turned out to be false—"although they only narrowly
escaped execution because of it"—and Elzbieta asks to be taken
to the man who was to have hidden her after Zofia. This tailor
(Tadeusz Lomnicki) refuses to speak with her about a past that
has scarred him, as he was the falsely accused victim.

The hands of the opening shot are as integral to *8* as those of
Tomek and Magda were to *6*. When we see the health-minded
Zofia exercising outdoors, the camera rests on a close-up of her
aging hands on a log. Elzbieta's own fingers are foregrounded in
the classroom when she plays with her gold chain, a cross dangling prominently. This image is profoundly ambiguous: has the
Jewish child become a Christian adult? (Zofia remarks to the class
that the visitor "works for an institute which researches the fate
of Jewish war survivors.") Or, given that Zofia later says to her,
"You are still alive. . . . How many times I must have seen
someone playing with a gold chain and thought . . . ," is Elzbieta's cross—the "lie" she had to wear in 1943—a ploy to jog the
professor's memory? After they get to the professor's apartment,

The tailor in *Decalogue, 8*

we also see Elzbieta's hands around the teacup Zofia offers her in the kitchen: since we know that the cold and thirsty little girl never had a chance to drink the tea prepared in 1943, a soothing ritual is enacted when Elzbieta finally gets to sip. Later, Zofia places her hand on the shoulder of the crying Elzbieta, who takes it into her own. At the very end, the tailor looks through his window at Zofia affectionately taking Elzbieta's hands.

The decision to end with this tailor adds a haunting

poignancy to *8*. Whereas the script closes with Zofia finding the priest who worked with her in the resistance during the war—to tell him the little girl is alive—the film deletes the scene, leaving us with a man who is unable to experience the catharsis allowed Zofia. The tailor certainly has his own story of betrayal and loss: perhaps more so than the female characters, he is the victim of the broken commandment "Thou shalt not bear false witness." Given that he was imprisoned in the 1950s on suspicion of having collaborated with the Gestapo, the tailor can be likened to the character played by the same actor in *Blind Chance*—the formerly jailed Communist Party veteran Werner. The tailor's refusal to speak about World War II brings to mind Elzbieta's provocative line earlier to Zofia, "We don't like witnesses to our humiliation." And if both women are shown trying to straighten a painting on Zofia's wall—which quickly returns to its crooked position—the tailor is a living reminder of how some things can't be fixed beyond a moment's change.

That he sees the women in the last shot through the bars of a window underlines his separation from healing contact. The pathos of his untold story is juxtaposed with the ability of Zofia and Elzbieta to move beyond the past. Kieslowski expresses their increasing understanding via lighting. After the class, the professor finds her visitor in the dark, deserted hallway. While they admit to being the figures from the story of 1943, the crosscutting keeps them separate; as in the cell sequence of *5* that isolates the lawyer and the criminal, the left half of Zofia's face is lit from the window, juxtaposed with the lit right half of Elzbieta's face.

They are then separated more definitively when Zofia drives to the building where the betrayal took place in 1943, and Elzbieta enters. Whereas the script simply shows her hiding in the courtyard for a moment—followed by Zofia looking worried before finding her—the film elaborates dramatically on the emotional subtext for both characters. In this nighttime scene, Elzbieta hides, which prompts Zofia to search for her; the professor goes upstairs and rings the doorbell of her former apartment. The disagreeable man who answers tells her five families are now living there, and—when she asks if Elzbieta was just there—dismisses her as a nutcase. A distraught Zofia finally finds Elzbieta in the car. Why this ruse? Elzbieta's vengeful hide-and-seek game has forced Zofia once again into the role of fearful protector.

Reliving the scene enables them to move on. At Zofia's apartment—where the professor fulfills an old promise of shelter—their extended conversation renders *8* the most blatantly philosophical and perhaps self-referential segment of *The Decalogue*. Already in the classroom scene, "ethical hell" was examined by a student telling the story of a woman whose husband is dying; pregnant with another man's child, she asks the doctor to tell her whether her husband will live—in which case she will have an abortion. We recognize the allusion to Dorota in *2,* and then Zofia tells the class that Warsaw is a small town: everyone knows that the husband lived—as did the child! Zofia is connected to the doctor of *2* because both have been confronted with a dilemma: can a person lie—should one bear false witness—to save the life of a child? She tells Elzbieta that she now believes "there is no idea or cause, nothing, more important than the life of a child."

The "angel," appearing in the classroom scene, contributes to this interconnectedness: while Elzbieta recounts the tale of the victimized Jewish girl, the camera pans from her face to that of the young man, who looks directly at the camera: his gaze—presumably at the professor—is quietly confrontational, creating visually a connection between Elzbieta's story and Zofia. He is indeed the silent witness to the professor's hidden humiliation. (His glance might be aimed at a larger Polish audience as well: given the classroom context, Kieslowski is perhaps alluding to the expulsion of Jewish students from Polish universities in 1968. He explained that the wartime context of *8* was indeed factual: "By chance, one of my friends told me the story of a Jewess to whom someone had promised help and who finally didn't give it. I understood that the subject was close to me, and that it wasn't bad to speak very naturally about Polish–Jewish relations in daily life without giving Polish or Jewish identity preponderant roles."[26])

But Zofia's remarks to Elzbieta in the apartment clarify what could not be spelled out in the classroom. They express not only her inherent decency but perhaps Kieslowski's vision of human beings. Using words remarkably similar to those of the director on pages 228–9 of *Kieslowski on Kieslowski,* Zofia invokes faith without reducing it to conventional terminology:

ZOFIA: About Good. I believe everyone has it in them. The world gives birth to either Good or Evil. That particular evening in 1943 did not bring out the Good in me.

ELZBIETA: And who is the judge of Good and Evil?

ZOFIA: He, who is in all of us.

ELZBIETA: I've never read anything in your work about God.

ZOFIA: I am reluctant to use the word 'God.' One can believe without having to use certain words. Man was created in order to choose . . . if so, perhaps we can leave God out of it.

ELZBIETA: And in his place?

ZOFIA: Here, on earth—solitude. And up there? If there really is no life after death, if there really is nothing, then . . .

Her voice trails off, leaving it to Elzbieta—as well as the viewer—to imagine the frightening void. It is hard not to see Zofia (whose name in Greek means wisdom) as Kieslowski's mouthpiece, espousing a skeptical humanism rooted in spiritual belief. It is perhaps shared by her visitor because, passing Elzbieta's door before she goes to sleep, Zofia sees her praying.

Elzbieta is consistent with Kieslowski's female characters in *2, 3, 4, 6,* and *7:* often young and confrontational, they push others around them to define their ethics. Like the pregnant Dorota, the suicidal Eva, the incestuously inclined Anka, the delusion-pricking Magda, or the rebellious Majka, Elzbieta seeks resolution. Whereas this resolution might be transient for the heroines of *3* or *7,* there is a genuine catharsis for the women of *8.* Zofia now knows that she was not responsible for the death of a child, and Elzbieta can now make sense of—and peace with—her childhood torment.

Decalogue, 9

If *8* is the most philosophical segment of *The Decalogue, 9* is the most Hitchcockian—a love story rooted in guilt and suspicion, expressed via objects charged with dramatic significance. Roman (Piotr Machalica), a middle-aged surgeon, learns that his recent impotence is incurable. Guilt-ridden and suicidal, he suggests a divorce to his wife Hanka (Eva Blaszczyk). With unwavering devotion, she refuses, insisting that love is in the heart, not between the legs. Roman spies on her and discovers Hanka's affair with a student, Mariusz.

Masochistically, he listens to her phone conversations and tails her, even to the apartment of Hanka's mother, which serves as the lovers' meeting place. Hidden inside a closet, he hears her telling Mariusz she doesn't want to see him again. Hanka discovers the bitterly embarrassed Roman but forgives him and suggests adopting a child. He says they need some time apart, and urges her to go skiing. But he glimpses Mariusz with skis and assumes they have arranged a rendezvous. When Mariusz surprises Hanka, she rushes back to Warsaw, fearful that Roman suspects a new betrayal. He has indeed tried to kill himself, but the last scene allows for cautious optimism: although badly injured, he calls her from a hospital, knowing Hanka's love for him has not wavered.

The crosscutting of the credit sequence connects Hanka—who sits up, startled, in the bed of their Warsaw apartment—with Roman, learning from a Kraków doctor that he will never be sexually active again. The montage suggests Hanka's deep love for her husband: she can sense when he is troubled, even at a distance. Hanka is then seen outside the apartment complex, but she suddenly returns upstairs to the phone. Whereas the screenplay fulfills her expectation—Roman does call—in the film she waits in vain by the phone. The film ends symmetri-

Piotr in *Decalogue, 9*

cally with Hanka agitatedly poised at the phone and finally rewarded with his call from the hospital.

The telephone, usually dominating the shot from the foreground, is a prominent character in *9*. As in Hitchcock's work—as well as the last sequence of Truffaut's Hitchcockian film, *The Soft Skin*—it seems to be capable of either destroying or saving a marriage as well as a life. Roman creates a secret way to listen in on Hanka's calls (preparing for the aural voyeurism of the Judge in *Red*) and then uses the phone to verify his suspicions: he calls the number he discovered rummaging through his wife's bag and learns that it belongs to Mariusz. Later, Hanka tries desperately to call Roman after her former lover turns up at the ski resort; but Roman is on his way out, having left a farewell note on the telephone. When she returns to the empty apartment, Hanka assumes it is too late and almost doesn't answer the ringing phone (which occupies a large por-

Hanka in *Decalogue, 9*

tion of screen space). The tension accumulates, until she finally picks it up.

Another revelatory object is the glove compartment of Roman's car, which often falls open without human intervention. Roman finds in it a physics notebook that belongs to Mariusz. Roman throws it into the garbage but then changes his mind: by this point, the book is filthy. He places it back in the glove compartment, and it is next seen at the apartment of

Hanka's tryst: freshly soiled by her husband, it becomes a sign for her that Roman has been perturbed by the notebook's presence. The visor of Roman's car functions symbolically when he glimpses Mariusz: lowering the visor, he enacts not only avoidance but the perhaps deluded idea that he won't be spotted if he can't see Mariusz.

Additional symbolic resonance is provided when Roman parks his car at the hospital. Alongside we see the hospital consultant who is having trouble pouring gas into his car with a funnel and petrol canister. The close-up of the funnel is blatantly phallic, a derisive reminder of Roman's impotence. Even the skis that Roman gets for his wife—and those he glimpses on Mariusz's car—acquire phallic connotation.

Among the dramatically charged objects in *9* are mirrors and glass reflectors. In the very first shot, the frightened Hanka sits up in bed and the camera pans to show her in the mirror; when Roman returns but can't bring himself to enter the building, she is seen waiting for him through the glass door; Roman is shown in the mirror once they are upstairs; when he hangs up the phone after hearing a young man ask for Hanka, we see his receding body through a glass dominating the foreground; arriving at Hanka's mother's apartment, Roman is presented from the very Hitchcockian perspective of an extreme low angle under a glass table; and we see his reflection in the bathroom mirror after he has witnessed Hanka and Mariusz leaving the apartment. These reflections prepare for the provocative doubling of two characters— Roman and Ola (Jolanta Pietek-Gorecka), a young patient endowed with a beautiful voice.

Ola is scheduled for elective heart surgery in order to be a singer. She tells Roman—for whom such a dangerous operation is usually a last resort—that she is happy with her current life, but her mother wishes her to be a famous singer, which Ola's weak heart will not permit. If Roman tempts fate by closing his eyes while driving the car, Ola does much the same thing with an operation that is not necessary. The weakness of her heart and that of Roman's loins lead to a shared question: is life worth living incompletely—minus something you think you must have? The film seems to endorse Hanka's observation to Roman, "the things we have are more important than the things we don't have."

Ola is the character who foregrounds music in 9, by telling Roman that she sings the work of the Dutch composer Van Den Budenmayer. Roman even buys the record and listens to it before Hanka comes home. Van Den Budenmayer is none other than Zbigniew Preisner, and the composer of *The Decalogue* weaves the music from Roman's record into the soundtrack of this segment.[27]

In the screenplay, Ola refers merely to Bach and Mahler when Roman asks her what she sings. The addition of Van Den Budenmayer to the film is one of many changes. Kieslowski deleted the first shot—Ania from 7 playing in the courtyard—preferring to jump right into the tense connection between Roman and Hanka. We no longer have the satiric jab at Polish waiting-in-line in the description of Ola's mother:

CONSULTANT: She stands for a living.
ROMAN: What do you mean, 'stands'?
CONSULTANT: She stands. You want a washing-machine, she'll stand in the queue for it. You need some furniture, she'll stand for you. Twenty-five per cent on top, but guaranteed delivery. (p. 246)

Instead, Kieslowski adds visually expressive images like the elevator in which Roman and Hanka go up to their apartment. During this dark and silent long take, the light is intermittent, alternating between illuminating her face and his. The elevator ride creates tension: even if they share the frame, the light separates them.

They are spatially separated when Roman hides in the apartment of Hanka's mother; but whereas the script has the camera discovering him after Hanka dismisses Mariusz, the film substitutes a subjective shot: we see from the point of view of the fearful husband rather than "objectively," and we identify with his effort to see even when Hanka walks out of the narrow frame. Tension is also added by a postcard that Mariusz sends Hanka: his love note is on the back of a picture of the Pope holding his fingers around his eyes like glasses. The comic portrait underlines voyeurism—which is precisely what Roman enacts when he finds the card in the mailbox of Hanka's mother.

Toward the end of the script, Roman drives off in his car and tries to kill himself. The film changes his instrument of attempted suicide into a bicycle: Roman is thus more vulnerable than in an enclosed vehicle. Moreover, after the bicycle topples over, Kieslowski remains on a close-up of the tire: it moves in one direction, then in the other, and stops. A shift in focus reveals the "angel" in the background, literally behind the turning spokes of the bicycle tire. (He has already been glimpsed on a bicycle after Roman learned his condition was incurable.) His presence at the two moments Roman "tempts fate" while driving seems magical indeed, as Roman does not succeed in dying either time.

The "angel" reminds us that *9* is connected to other parts of *The Decalogue,* to Kieslowski's subsequent films, and perhaps to his own life. As in *2,* the husband's recovery is miraculous, and a couple will re-form despite the man's hospitalization and the wife's adultery. As in *6,* the male character is a voyeur whose tormented love for a woman leads him to spy on her. Moreover, when Hanka is trying to end the relationship with Mariusz and says crisply to him, "Do up your jacket and leave," she seems as cold as Magda dismissing Tomek after their sexual encounter. But a more intriguing connection can be made between *9* and *1,* because the film adds two lines to the end of the screenplay: when Hanka hears Roman's voice on the phone, she says, "God, you're there," and Roman replies, "I'm here." Is she merely addressing her husband? Or is she invoking God as well? After all, much like Pawel's aunt vis-à-vis Krzysztof in the first segment, Hanka has been counteracting Roman's belief in medical statistics with her own faith. (Although Roman does not seem religious, only he wears a conspicuous cross on his neck.)

More than other segments, *9* lays the groundwork for Kieslowski's next films. On a stylistic level, the vital camera of Piotr Sobocinski—who would go on to shoot *Red*—narrates the story with a life of its own. When Roman hums a few bars of Van Den Budenmayer in his office, the camera pans left so that he is partially obscured by shelves in the left foreground. As with other shots that relegate him to the background, this visual strategy is a graphic reminder of Roman's weakness. After Hanka discovers him spying in her mother's closet, the sequence ends with the camera panning right: the effect is that of a curtain moving left, as increasing darkness overtakes the characters. When Roman rides his bicycle off the cliff, the camera recedes from his inert body to the broken white line of the highway, evoking how the heart rate is recorded on a hospital monitor.

On a thematic level, the impotent and humiliated Roman is a cinematic brother to Karol in *White*. And in addition to his telephonic connection to the Judge in *Red,* his suicide attempts prefigures that of Julie in *Blue*. One can find in *Decalogue, 9* a central theme of the trilogy—the regenerative power of love. But it also contains a blueprint of *The Double Life of Veronique,* as Ola is obviously an embryonic version of Veronika. In the screenplay of *The Decalogue,* we are led to understand that Ola died from the heart surgery:

CONSULTANT: Upset about the young girl? What was her name—Ola?
ROMAN: Ola Jarek. Yes—
CONSULTANT: No one could have predicted she would—
ROMAN: I know. But I'd still like fewer operations. (p. 271)

It is unclear who operated on her, and precisely how (or if) she died. This scene—which does not appear in the film—foreshadows the director's own death. Kieslowski willingly went to the Warsaw hospital for heart surgery and died there after the operation. In retrospect, Ola is a deeply troubling double not only for Roman but for the filmmaker.

Decalogue, 10

If *1* as well as *9* are among the darkest emotional explorations of the *Decalogue, 10* is the lightest. Although the action is engendered by a death—of the man who proudly showed Zofia three "Polarfahrt/Zeppelin" stamps in *8*—the credit sequence establishes the ironically upbeat tone of the final segment. Artur (Zbigniew Zamachowski) sings with his rock band, "City Death," lyrics that invoke the Ten Commandments:

> *Kill, kill, kill*
> *Screw who you will*
> *Lust and crave*
> *Pervert and deprave*
> *Every day of the week*
> *Every day of the week*
> *On Sunday hit mother*
> *Hit father, hit brother*
> *Hit sister, the weakest*
> *And steal from the meekest*
> *'Cos everything's yours*
> *Yeah, everything's yours. (p. 298)*

His brother Jerzy (Jerzy Stuhr) tries to get his attention: their father has died. Whereas the script begins with the funeral, the film moves first from the rock concert to the father's apartment, where a shot of dead fish in a tank sets a grimly comic tone. (The tone, and the tank, remain throughout, as the brothers never throw out the sickly green water.) At the funeral, Artur's Walkman continues to play rock music while a man makes a speech about "Root," whose obsession was collecting stamps, "a noble passion."

The brothers are stunned to learn that their father's collection is worth a fortune. But they are stumped in their effort to

Jerzy and Artur in *Decalogue, 10*

sell it because Artur pulled out the three "Zeppelins"—ignorant of their worth—for Jerzy to give his young son who likes airplanes. They go to great lengths to protect the collection, including the acquisition of an enormous dog for security. When it turns out they can obtain a rare stamp that their father coveted, the deal is severe: in exchange, Jerzy will have to donate a kidney to save the stamp merchant's daughter. He does so, but their father's apartment is robbed at the same time. In the end—after suspecting each other of the theft—all they have is their new-found trust as well as a passion for stamps.

Zbigniew Preisner's music is intrusive in *10,* partly because of eerie percussive effects that accompany the brothers' growing realization of their father's fortune. It begins with timpani drums when they (and the camera) approach the tank with dead fish floating, and returns when Artur takes a sample of the collection to experts. When, after the robbery, each of them sees three suspicious individuals greeting each other—the man who claimed their father owed him money, the youth who exchanged the "Zeppelins" for worthless stamps, and the merchant—the drum sounds function like a throbbing awakening: both of the older men have black dogs just like their "security" animal, who was made to sit quietly during the robbery!

This scene, which does not appear in the script, opens up the possibility that the brothers will locate the criminals and get their collection back. And whereas the screenplay ends with Jerzy and Artur finding each other in the post office—and buying new stamps together—the film ends in the apartment, each of them realizing they bought the same new stamps. With appropriate symmetry, the apartment complex that anchors all ten segments becomes the setting for the closing scene. And the last words—as the brothers lay out three stamps each—are, self-consciously enough, "a series!" The "Kill, kill" rock song returns for the final credits, ending not only *10* but *The Decalogue* with an ironic undercutting of its very tenets.

The irony is especially pungent in the way Kieslowski cross-cuts the kidney operation and the robbery: whereas the script presents events sequentially, the film's montage juxtaposes two operations that are intended to remove something. And if the script includes a few scenes of Jerzy's irritated wife—including her asking for a divorce—the film deletes her presence after a cursory introduction. Indeed, many of the changes from the screenplay streamline events to focus on the relationship between the brothers, who have not seen each other in two years. Had Jerzy's wife remained equally present, *10* would have resembled *Camera Buff*, in which the same actor incarnates a man who loses his wife and child because of a new obsession. Kieslowski also deleted reference to the father's political past, as in *7:* only the script mentions that "Root" was imprisoned in the early 1950s (like the tailor of *8*) after having been in the Home Army.

What he adds to the script is primarily visual. For example, when the brothers meet the stamp dealer in the park, the camera is positioned behind a tree: it is clearly a point-of-view shot, suggesting that someone is watching them. Although we don't get to see who is spying in the park, voyeurism is invoked in the post office: Tomek, the "Peeping Tom" from *6,* is the one who sells Jerzy the stamps. Alive and well at the end of *The Decalogue,* he is perhaps a substitute for the "angel," who seems to have no place in the relatively comic frame of "not coveting thy neighbor's goods."

Tomek's presence is a reminder of the interconnected quality of *The Decalogue*—the fact that this cinematic whole is greater than the sum of its parts. And Kieslowski's reticence about labeling a segment as illustrating a particular commandment reflects his own understanding of the moral principles articulated in Exodus 20: 2–17: the whole of the Ten Commandments is greater than the sum of its parts. Each segment of *The Decalogue* invokes a number of commandments, and *10* takes on almost all of them. Given the complexity of life at the end of the twentieth century, no one commandment can exist without reference to the others, just as no human being can live fully in isolation. Kieslowski's ten short films about mor(t)ality don't so much illustrate as interrogate the commandments. They ask of the viewer lucidity and compassion—both in the watching of *The Decalogue* and in our lives. "Everyone seems to accept the Ten Commandments as a kind of moral basis," the director observed, "and everyone breaks them daily. Just the attempt to respect them is already a major achievement. If I had to formulate the message of my 'Decalogue,' I'd say, 'Live carefully, with your eyes open, and try not to cause pain.' "[28]

CHAPTER FIVE

The Double Life of Veronique

The Double Life of Veronique (1991) is a magnificently reflexive film in every sense of the term. Reflections in glass abound—appropriate to the story of two young women living parallel lives in contemporary Poland and France. Like much of Kieslowski's previous work, it is a gently self-conscious meditation on looking as well as storytelling—in other words, on filmmaking. This French–Polish co-production invites the viewer to reflect on the threads that bind each of us to forces outside ourselves. "A metaphysical thriller" is how the producer Leonardo de la Fuente pungently described the film, whose screenplay was co-written by Krzysztof Piesiewicz. The work of Kieslowski's previous collaborators such as cinematographer Slawomir Idziak and composer Zbigniew Preisner is equally integral to *The Double Life of Veronique:* the images seem bathed in gold, while the sumptuous original music links the two heroines.

Both are played by newcomer Irene Jacob, who—after learning Polish for the film—won the Best Actress Award at the 1991 Cannes Film Festival. Although Kieslowski initially wanted Andie MacDowell for the part(s)—having admired her performance in *sex, lies and videotape* when he was on the jury of the 1989 Cannes Film Festival where Soderbergh's film was in competition—he realized that a European actress would be more credible. Jacob, a young French-Swiss actress, had appeared briefly as the piano teacher in *Au Revoir les Enfants,* which Kieslowski loved. During one of his seminars, he asked his students how many remembered seeing a young woman in Louis Malle's film. When the majority raised their hands, he understood that—despite less than two minutes of screen time—Jacob made an impression. He screen-tested her, in addition to numerous French actresses, and was not only impressed by her talent but touched by her shyness: "It's rare to see timid, reserved people in this business," he added.[1]

In Poland, Veronika is a warm-hearted singer living with her widowed father (Wladyslaw Kowalski, who also played the father in *Decalogue, 7*). She goes to Kraków and wins a competition to sing the haunting piece of music by Van Den Budenmayer (the composer invoked in *Decalogue, 9,* but in reality

Irene Jacob in *The Double Life of Veronique*

Preisner). Despite the warning of a mild heart attack, she performs triumphantly but then suddenly collapses and dies before the concert is over.

In Clermont-Ferrand, Veronique inexplicably decides to give up her singing career. She too has a heart problem and devotes herself to teaching music to young children. At her school, she is drawn to a marionette artist and author of children's books, Alexandre Fabbri (Philippe Volter). The star of his spectacle is a ballerina puppet, who performs, falls, and is resurrected as a butterfly. Veronique receives a mysterious phone call—including a tape of the Polish Veronika singing Van Den Budenmayer—and two enigmatic packages: one is a shoelace, the other a cassette of sounds that seem to have been recorded at a train station. She follows these clues to the Gare Saint-Lazare in Paris, where Alexandre is indeed waiting for her.

He tells Veronique that he wanted to see if it was psychologically possible for a woman to follow the "call of the unknown." Distraught at the notion that she is merely being used for his next book, she runs away. But Alexandre finds her in a Paris hotel. Pointing to her contact sheet of photos taken in Kraków he says, "Look at you." Realizing it is not her, Veronique begins to cry—which is precisely when Alexandre kisses her and turns the tears into an orgasm; because the photo of Veronika is intercut with their lovemaking, it seems to include her double. At Alexandre's home, he recites to Veronique his new story, about the parallel life of two women born in 1966.

Why a puppeteer as the link between the women? Kieslowski felt he needed something delicate as well as mysterious, and he remembered seeing an American marionettist named Bruce Schwartz on Japanese television: "He was a miracle-worker. He shows his hands, he moves with the puppet, and three seconds later you forget the hands because the puppet really begins to live."[2] (It is indeed Schwartz's hands that we see during Alexandre's act.) But, more so than in his previous films, Kieslowski centers the narrative on a woman and leads us to identify with her through a combination of subjective camera

English STOP sign in Poland

and close-ups. The two heroines are obviously an elaboration of Ola, the secondary character in *Decalogue, 9* who chooses risky heart surgery in order to sing. And when the French Veronique is introduced having a premonition that someone close to her just died, she can be likened to such characters as the wife in *Camera Buff* or Hanka in *Decalogue, 9,* who have an uncanny way of sensing trouble at a distance. Even more than Urszula in *No End,* Kieslowski's new heroines seem to live with a delicate string that links them to the unknown.

The opening sequence presents visual keys to unlock the meaning of *The Double Life of Veronique.* In 1968 Poland,[3] the upside-down image of a dark street turns out to be the perspective of two-year-old Veronika: the Polish voice-over of her mother asks her to look for the stars on this winter night, almost Christmas Eve. The next shot reveals the child pointing up, her mother's hands holding her so that she can see beyond traditional perspective. Cut to 1968 France, where a child's eye dominates the frame: as the magnifying glass is removed from before her face, we see that the act of looking is once again the concern of the shot. The mother's French voice-over invites the child to examine a leaf, and we hear the sound of birds. It is a spring day, which means that the film's first two scenes are not simultaneous: the experiences of the Polish Veronika precede— and perhaps prepare for—those of the French Veronique.

Both of these opening images connect the little girl to the physical universe. If a leaf is explored at the opening, Veronique places her hand on a tree in the last scene: as she is about to see her beloved papa, touching the trunk suggests that her warm and open character is rooted in the affections of a solid father, as well as an appreciation of terrestrial continuity. And in addition to this visual rhyme, Kieslowski includes the proliferation of dead leaves when Veronika has a mild heart attack in the street.

The unseen mother is the guide at the opening, making her daughter aware of the physical world. (However, the French mother's voice seems to be that of Irene Jacob, suggesting that the opening is a subjective flashback from the grown

Veronika singing in the rain, *The Double Life of Veronique*

Veronique's point of view.) "Look," says the mother in both scenes—preparing for how Alexandre will become Veronique's guide to another dimension: "Look," he says about the contact sheet and, metaphorically, her double existence. The audience tries to look at the heroine in the film's third introduction of the title character, but Kieslowski continues his questioning of sight itself: during the credit sequence, the image of the young woman is distorted, as if a magnifying glass were attached to the lens. The periphery of the frame is fuzzy, as in the France '68 opening. She seems to be walking in a sunny street and then dropping her music folder. (Is this a flash-forward to the Kraków demonstration scene, in which Veronika drops the folder?) The act of looking is foregrounded because we are not sure of what we are seeing.

The adult Veronika is finally presented clearly after the credits, singing exuberantly outdoors as the rain begins. She looks upward, as in the opening shot. (The skyward glance will also be her final look, since Kieslowski presents Veronika's funeral

from the low-angle point of view of the glass-topped coffin.)
Whereas the other young female singers behind her cower from
the rain, Veronika holds the last note, her smiling face welcoming the raindrops. Seeing her openness to water, we are
reminded of her elemental connections to air and earth as a
child. Similarly, when she gets the music score in Kraków,
Veronika looks up and welcomes a light shower of orange dust
from a ceiling tapped by her ball. Her elemental ties include
fire: it exists not only in the golden tones of the cinematography[4], but in her own glowing sexuality. In the next scene, she
kisses her boyfriend Antek passionately amid the pelting drops,
and then makes love with him in her apartment. During the
frankly erotic scene—her openness to physicality includes the
flesh—Veronika looks at a large photo of herself on the wall;
this will be rhymed by the inclusion of a photo of Veronika
when Alexandre and Veronique consummate their passion in
Paris. Moreover, our first glimpse of the French heroine is in
bed with her boyfriend; suddenly, she withdraws, as if sensing
that someone close to her is dead.

The doubling exists on a variety of levels, explicit and
implicit. Both heroines are sensuous with their lovers, affectionate with their kind fathers, and prone to rubbing their
lower eyelids with a ring. They are left-handed, wear red
gloves, and notice old women who walk with difficulty
(Veronika when she is getting dressed for the concert and yells
to a woman that she can carry her bags, and Veronique during
her class). Each is seen with objects including lip balm, a little
plastic ball that reflects, and string: Veronika twists a piece of
string from her music folder until it snaps, and Veronique
receives a shoelace in the mail. When she holds it straight
against her electrocardiogram report from the hospital, the
image of the taut line suggests death[5]—rhyming with the string
that dangles momentarily above Veronika's coffin. Each has a
weak heart, a beautiful voice, and a predilection for the music
of Van Den Budenmayer. Veronique dreams of the landscape
that Veronika's father was painting. Eastern and Western Euro-

pean versions of the same character, one travels from a Polish province to Kraków, the other from Clermont-Ferrand to Paris.

Even Alexandre's work requires two puppets of the same character. At his home, Veronique discovers him making a marionette of her. "Why two?" she asks. "Because I touch them a lot during the show, and one might be damaged," he replies. And his spectacle is about doubling: the ballerina wants to dance, seems to die (although Veronique later says the ballerina simply broke her leg), and reemerges as a butterfly. Is Veronique able to fly precisely because Veronika falls? Is the death of the Polish woman a warning to her French counterpart to stop singing? Kieslowski includes a strange image after Alexandre first calls Veronique: she seems to see Veronika singing on the Polish stage and collapsing against a red background. The film's central question seems to be blatantly metaphysical: can there be—in God's spectacle, which includes individual "damage"—a double who prepares us for survival? Or might some of us be the double who is setting the stage for another to live more wisely?

The doubling extends to that of Alexandre and the filmmaker. This magician is first seen amid lighting equipment at the school—like a director—and then tells his story via images of transformation. As Joanna Present, a Barnard College student, wrote in an unpublished manuscript:

> Kieslowski's recurring emphasis on doubling, through both fate and art, is an allegorical reflection of the film medium. In film, lives are artificially doubled on celluloid; the lives the audience witnesses are ghosts, chemical indices of what has passed before the camera.

Alexandre is an omniscient manipulator, as when his van pulls up alongside Veronique while she is lighting a cigarette from the wrong end. He seems related to the "angel" in *The Decalogue:* one never knows where he will turn up and how he might be

Alexandre's puppets, *The Double Life of Veronique*

connected to events. Alexandre can also be connected to Tomek in *A Short Film about Love:* each spies on the woman he desires, using the phone and the mail to get closer to her.

Ultimately, and perhaps like Kieslowski, Alexandre's love

for Veronique coexists with his exploitation of her. She ru..s from him at the train station because she fears that his interest in her is schematic, to serve his book.[6] He later convinces her otherwise, but in their last scene together, he has indeed made a puppet of her image and written a text that—as he puts it— could be titled "The Double Life of . . . ." Like the director, he places the birth of his characters in 1966 and details the early connections between the little girls; for example, one burns herself, and then the other instinctively recoils from the flame. Although he is the seductive agent of heightened perception— perhaps an evolved soul—he is finally abandoned by Veronique when she senses his poaching of her life for his own creative ends. Kieslowski seems to be questioning the combination of talent, love, opportunism, and perhaps guilt of the storyteller who uses real lives in his art.

These reflections are visually grounded in the film's use of glass. The magnifying lens before the eye in "France, 1968" continues with the introduction of Veronika's father in profile, behind the round frame of his eyeglasses; nearby, Veronika speaks to him, reflected in her window at night. When she takes the train to Kraków, we see the landscape through the slight distortion of the window and then through the refracted light of her plastic ball. In Kraków, Veronika is reflected in a mirror when she is on the phone and in a window at the back of a bus as Antek drives on his motorcycle behind her. Her funeral is presented through a glass-covered coffin: as handfuls of earth are thrown down, the point of view is obscured.

In France, Veronique stares at Alexandre's reflection during his show and is then reflected herself in the window of the bookstore where she sees his volumes displayed. The next shot is an enigmatic glass of tea, the bag dancing in the water (unlike Kieslowski's earlier heroines, Veronique will not let it fall). She uses a magnifying lens to decipher that the stamps on the envelope containing the cassette came from the Gare Saint-Lazare (recalling the child's magnifying glass of the opening). At the station, she hovers behind the swinging glass door of the café, whose reflec-

The last shots of *The Double Life of Veronique*

tion reveals the table where Alexandre has been waiting. (Significantly enough, the window next to him affords a view of a decimated car outside: the sounds of a crash and an ambulance were on the cassette, suggesting that death is ever present.) Finally, the last shot of *The Double Life of Veronique* shows her hugging her father outdoors through a window—both on screen right and screen left! The image is parallel rather than reflected, suggesting two different daughters embracing their fathers.

It is noteworthy that Kieslowski added this ending for American audiences after the film's U.S. premiere at the New York Film Festival. As Harvey Weinstein, co-chairman of Miramax—the U.S. distributor for *The Double Life of Veronique*—recalled in *Premiere*, Kieslowski hoped to clarify the ending: "We sat in a hotel room and Krzysztof drew storyboards for me on hotel stationery of the changes he wanted to make. We brought in the footage from Poland and, using Krzysztof's storyboards, made the changes."[7] The last shot of the French version merely shows Veronique placing her hand on the tree before her father's house. Kieslowski envisioned other possible endings, including Veronique going to Kraków and seeing a third image of herself. Because the film was opening in seventeen Paris theaters, he even expressed the desire to have seventeen different versions playing simultaneously! As he elaborated in *Télérama*, "There would have been numbers for each version. I was quite serious about it, but didn't have enough time to make it work. I think some viewers would have had as much fun with this as me."[8] And if he generally made eight or nine versions of a film, *The Double Life of Veronique* required twenty "because the subject was difficult and delicate."[9]

After an abundance of upside-down images, the two existing endings present solidity through verticality. Veronique and her father are standing as straight as the tree, which brings to mind Kieslowski's repeated mention of an "inner compass" that clearly points you in a certain direction. Nevertheless, the representation of their embrace—like the last shot of *No End*, in which the ghosts of Urszula and her husband recede through a window—requires a "double take" from the viewer: the ambiguity of precisely what we are seeing is as great as that of the opening shot of *The Double Life of Veronique*.

To this very first shot of horizontal reversal—Veronika seeing the sky from bottom up—Kieslowski adds the little plastic ball that reflects (reminiscent of the circular ornaments on

Kieslowski with Irene Jacob, shooting *The Double Life of Veronique*

Magda's window in *A Short Film about Love*): the ball, both in Poland and France, includes a church seen upside down. This 180-degree turn is enacted when Veronika collapses onstage, and again during Veronique's love scene with Alexandre: as she awakens in the hotel bed, he positions himself above her head, upside down, before kissing her. And when she climaxes with him, the camera assumes the same position above her ecstatic face: we see Veronique the way Veronika saw heaven. Similarly, Kieslowski often shows the heroines from a 45-degree angle: Veronika is depicted horizontally when talking to her aunt in Kraków, and after the heart pain in the street. (Curiously enough, it is from her inverted point of view after the malaise that we see a well-dressed man walking past her and briefly exposing himself!)

Veronique's head is also somewhat to the side in one of the film's most haunting scenes: she has been napping in her loft and is awakened by the play of golden light entering her window. Searching for the source, she notices a little boy moving a mirror from his window across the street. Like Veronique, we assume that the shimmering light comes from the child's playful and intermittent reflections of the sun. But after he goes inside and closes his window, the light continues, as piercingly beautiful and inexplicable as the music we have been hearing. After all, the film's score begins diegetically too, traceable to a source: the choral music during the credits turns out to be sung by Veronika in the rainy street. But Preisner's melodies continue like magical aural strings between the two women, invoking invisible forces at work. The scene ends, appropriately enough, with the light directing Veronique toward the string of her music folder.

As in *Decalogue, 9,* Kieslowski winks at the audience by having Veronique tell her class that their music was written two hundred years ago by a Dutch composer: the name Van Den Budenmayer is visible on the blackboard. The children struggle to play on their instruments the very piece that Veronika died singing. Alexandre hears the class through the window, which explains why he would play the recording of Veronika's swan song on the phone to Veronique: the music is already familiar to the French teacher.

It was Preisner's idea to use Dante's poetry in old Italian as lyrics in composing the music. *The Double Life of Veronique* (whose original title was *The Choirgirl*) begins with the central melody played on flute and then introduces the choral segment during the credits. The dramatically integrated score deepens when Veronika sits in on a rehearsal for which her friend is the accompanist: spontaneously and beautifully, she sings along with the male choir. The woman who has been conducting subsequently introduces Veronika to the conductor (Aleksander Bardini) who is in charge of the competition. They have discovered their star because the music of Van Den Budenmayer/Preisner was a magnet to her voice. The orchestration is noteworthy during the concert sequence: there are two female soloists, and Veronika's voice intertwines harmoniously with a kind of musical double. Both voices carry the melody amid the support of the orchestra—suggestive, perhaps, of a soul making its way through life.

The soundtrack fulfills Piesiewicz's observation at the 1997 Paris colloquium, "We wanted to make a film about nostalgia, its mystery—the yearning for love, for art, for closeness." Preisner's music in *The Double Life of Veronique* also prepares for *Blue:* his composition not only is sung by Veronika but virtually represents her after death. In Kieslowski's next film, music is once again a reminder of the heroine's double—or other life—namely, that of her past self.

CHAPTER SIX

Three Colors: Blue

God loves a trinity.

—Russian toast
for the third drink

JUST AS the inspiration for *The Decalogue* came from Krzysztof Piesiewicz, so the idea for *Three Colors* originated with Kieslowski's co-writer. "One night, I saw a Polish composer being interviewed on television," Piesiewicz told *Télérama*. "He was with his wife. I said to myself that this woman must have an important role in his life. This was the starting point for 'Blue,' which is a film about freedom."[1] And if *The Decalogue* cinematically redefined the Ten Commandments from lofty abstractions into the daily decisions of ordinary people, the trilogy likewise transmutes the colors of the French flag—as well as the concepts of liberty, equality, and fraternity—into very personal and complex arenas.

Kieslowski and Piesiewicz were joined by the legendary French producer Marin Karmitz, who oversaw the production of these three films that constitute such a singular and rich mosaic. Set, respectively, in Paris, Warsaw, and Geneva, *Blue, White,* and *Red* were shot in a staggeringly short period: the first was filmed between September and November of 1992, and the rest of the trilogy was shot by May of 1993. By September, *Blue* had won the prize for Best Film at the 1993 Venice Film Festival, as well as Best Actress for Juliette Binoche.

Blue is emotionally dark, visually haunting, and musically ravishing. Cinematographer Slawomir Idziak and composer Zbigniew Preisner are as central to *Blue* as they were to *The Double Life of Veronique*. In addition to his recognizable use of filters and camera-on-shoulder, Idziak is even credited as "Screenplay Collaborator" (along with Kieslowski's friends Agnieszka Holland and Edward Zebrowski). Preisner composed the entire score before shooting began: the music is thus a "pre-text," its melodies, textures, and rhythms engendering action. Because the main characters are indeed composers, the score is part of the plot, and its authorship part of the film's mystery.

Blue begins with a car crash in which Julie (Binoche) loses her husband Patrice, a famous composer, and her little daughter. When she learns of their death while recovering in the hospital, Julie tries to kill herself. Unable to end her life, she at least puts an end to her past: Julie gives orders to sell their house and everything in it, destroys Patrice's almost-finished score, sleeps with Olivier (Benoit Régent)—her husband's collaborator, who worships her—as a kind of farewell, and moves to an anonymous life in Paris. Although she tries to live without history or desire, memories surface: bits of music overcome her, accompanied by blackouts that return to the same shot. The theme of oblivion is enriched by Julie's visits to her mother in a nursing home. Played by Emmanuelle Riva—whose very presence invokes *Hiroshima, Mon Amour,* where she starred as the woman obsessed by the fear of forgetting—the mother cannot remember who Julie is.[2]

Julie is befriended by Lucille (Charlotte Very), a neighbor whom other tenants want to evict for "loose" morals. Heeding Lucille's plea to come to the strip club where she works, Julie accidentally sees on a TV screen a story about her husband and learns that he had a mistress. She finds the young woman, Sandrine (Florence Pernel), who is pregnant with Patrice's child. She also realizes that Olivier has a copy of her husband's unfinished score. Julie begins returning to an engaged life, first by resuming work on Patrice's music with Olivier, and then by offering her old house to Patrice's mistress, as well as the family name for the unborn child. In the last scene, her lovemaking with Olivier seems more like renewal than farewell.

From the very first shots, *Blue* is intricately structured, aurally as well as visually. It introduces key images that accumulate meaning throughout the film and makes us aware of what we cannot see as well as what is revealed. Sound precedes picture, as we hear a car before the black screen reveals movement on a road: the camera is positioned behind the wheel of a fast-moving vehicle, creating a precarious feeling. This is the first of numerous changes from the screenplay, which begins with an establishing shot of the busy highway before the camera descends to pick out the navy blue BMW. Indeed, most of the changes are deletions: Kieslowski kept cutting for dramatic compression, retaining only the essential scenes, characters, and images.

The second shot fuses the crackling noise of a candy wrapper with the image of a hand extending this blue paper out the window of a blue car, held up to the sky. A little girl is seen through the window of the back seat, circular lights intermittently flashing. The fourth shot is her point of view in a tunnel. After the car stops so that she can relieve herself outside, we see a close-up of oil dripping from a tube in the car, a detail that elicits suspense.

In the next—and equally abstracted—shot, a hand attempts to get a ball onto a stick. We then see that the hand belongs to a young man seated by the highway, who watches the blue car pass. It is precisely when he succeeds in getting the ball onto the stick, and smiles, that we hear the crash. After the primarily horizontal movement of the opening shots, the verticality of the stick game prepares for the shot of a tree on which the wrecked car is mounted. As this young man, Antoine (Yann Tregouet), runs to the car, the child's beach ball rolls away from the accident, rhyming with his ball. Although Antoine is merely a witness, the eerie coincidence of his game and the crash raises the question of whether he could be some messenger of fate. ("This happened to me," Kieslowski revealed. "I was the witness of a similar accident, hence this boy."[3]) Alternatively, since a brief shot of his outstretched thumb suggests he might have been hitchhiking, would the car have crashed if they had stopped to pick him up?

That we see Antoine's ball while hearing the accident renders the soundtrack dramatically potent. Kieslowski, working with sound engineer Jean-Claude Laureux, heightens sounds throughout *Blue:* he even asked Laureux to imply a car crash when the door later slams in Julie's Paris apartment.[4] Our first image of Julie in the hospital is aural, consisting of her labored breath as feathers in close-up move to the rhythm of her respiration. Other striking sounds in *Blue* include the crash of the piano lid before Julie leaves the family home; the increasingly louder knocking on doors of a man in her apartment house, who is fleeing attackers in the middle of the night; the wind closing the door behind her when she ventures out on the landing to see if the man has escaped; the squeal of baby mice in Julie's closet, which frightens her—much like the subsequent squealing of little girls jumping into a swimming pool, suggesting that Julie's fear might be of babies rather than animals; and the enhanced slamming of the door once she has placed a neighbor's cat in the closet with the mice.

From the very first shot of the film, sound is associated with circularity, as the rumble turns out to be from a speeding tire on a road. Circular images recur not only in the direct presentation of Antoine's stick game and Anna's beach ball but in the music scores that are rolled up at the copyist's office: Kieslowski shoots Julie from behind a row of rolled-up scores, creating a series of iris effects that isolate the character. We later see, from her point of view in a café, part of a round coffee cup as the light fades; this shot is visually rhymed with a subsequent circular image in the café when Julie looks at her reflection in a bright spoon. She is seen through the round window of the courtroom when she searches for Sandrine, who is a lawyer. But the most intriguing circle she encounters might be the chain found by Antoine in the crash and later returned to her. When Julie and Antoine meet, a rack focus shifts attention from the round necklace—a gold cross dangling—to Julie; although it was a gift to her from Patrice, she insists that Antoine keep it.

Circularity is appropriate to a film in which the heroine tries to live with metaphorical blinders: looking only at what is ahead, Julie is nevertheless brought back to what is behind her. The splashes of blue, combined with music, express the return of the repressed—that which Julie must sooner or later confront— whether it is grief or need for another human being. Blue is associated with her daughter from the beginning via the lollipop wrapper held out the car window; Julie subsequently finds another such lollipop in her bag and chews the blue candy with a frightening ferocity. (Ingesting it rather than throwing it away suggests a bizarre communion.) She later asks if the "blue room" has been emptied: it is indeed her daughter's, and the sole item that remains is the child's chandelier hanging from the ceiling.

Bits of blue and white glass dangle from this circular mobile: Julie tries to pull it down but succeeds only in grasping a few beads. When she sits on the steps, light from an unseen source flickers over her eyes; we later realize that it is the reflection of the beads in her palm. The mobile is the only thing she takes to Paris with her. A continuing emblem of her daughter, the chandelier again creates a play of light on Julie's face, reflecting the sun that enters her apartment. In a haunting return, bits of blue light are superimposed on her closed eyes when she is accidentally locked out of her apartment in the middle of the night and must wait seated on the stairs. When she decides at the end of *Blue* to go to Olivier, we see Julie through the blue light of the mobile. Beautiful as well as painful, this arrangement of glass tearlike shapes is an objective correlative of memory.

The color blue permeates the film in a number of ways. There are literal images, like her being dressed "black and blue" when she arrives in Paris—blue jeans, black jacket and T-shirt— or Julie's blue ink when writing music. The copyist notes that the unfinished concerto has many corrections: these are indeed Julie's "blue" notes, whose round shape visually echoes the beads of the mobile. The figurative use of blue can be seen in the enormous pool where Julie often swims alone: the placid blue surface initially suggests escape, but it is precisely in the water that she twice gasps and stops, suddenly overcome by fragments of the unfinished concerto. With the accompanying blackouts, the pool symbolizes incomplete mourning as the space where Julie opts for physical exertion rather than emotional confrontation of loss. The swimming pool is visually connected to the television screen, another blue surface that can function as either escape or reflection of grief. The first TV is a miniature placed next to her head in the hospital, enabling Julie to watch the funeral of her husband and daughter. In extreme close-up, she touches the screen, her finger larger than the tiny coffins.

The television to which her mother is glued has a brighter tone, maybe because she watches "escapist" images: when Julie first visits her, the program shows an old man bungee-jumping (rhyming with the bungee-jumper that preceded the funeral on Julie's miniature TV); attached to a rope, the elderly diver plummets downward, is seen upside down, and then defies gravity by returning up. Perhaps Kieslowski chose this modern sport because its circularity and elasticity represent the ultimate resiliency of life within Julie. The second time she visits, her mother's television set presents a tightrope walker. These risky images coexist with the "safe" space around the older woman: whenever Julie approaches, we see glass protectively framing the mother. She may be hiding from the past too: their first interchange—in which she calls her daughter Marie-France—establishes that her sister is dead. Is this why the mother won't remember? Both generations seem to evade—through isolation—mourning the death of a beloved family member.

The reflections that proliferate at the nursing home—which graphically embody the mother's confusion about whether Julie is Marie-France—are part of a pattern of imagery throughout *Blue*. As in Kieslowski's previous films, the presence of glass and other reflecting surfaces foregrounds the theme of vision. Although the characters of his trilogy may never be completely "free, equal, or fraternal," they can approach a lucidity that

Julie's mother plus reflection, *Blue*

equips them to live. This is no less true for the audience, who Kieslowski leads to fulfill a precept articulated in *Hiroshima, Mon Amour*: "The art of seeing has to be learned," says the character played by Emmanuelle Riva. Resnais's film, like the *Three Colors* trilogy, probes sight that is not simply apprehension but comprehension, not recognition but revelation. An example in *Blue* might be the shot of Julie dipping a white sugar cube into coffee and then holding it above the cup: the extreme close-up of the cube getting dark is not simply of phenomenological interest, but suggests an "infusion" of life that is taking place in Julie. (Kieslowski, however, proposed the opposite interpretation in the 1994 French TV interview: "The sugar cube shows that she cares about nothing beyond her.")

Glass is problematic for the heroine at the beginning of *Blue*: she smashes the hallway window of the hospital in order to divert the nurse's attention. Julie then steals pills, tries to swallow a handful, and stops when she sees the nurse looking at her through another window. Glass is absurdly reductive when she sees the funeral on the tiny screen. It becomes more expressive of Julie as she is about to leave her home: having invited Olivier to the now-empty house on a stormy night, she tells him to undress. On Julie's face is the reflection of the rain from the window, a blue-green image that takes the place of the tears she cannot shed. (When Julie asks her maid why she is sobbing, the old woman answers, "because you aren't.")

The glass around her mother's room embodies the distance not only between them, but within each of these women: the mother's discontinuous relationship to her own past—a medical phenomenon like Alzheimer's—is mirrored in Julie's willed dissociation from her own history. But when Julie visits Lucille at the peep show, Kieslowski uses glass—as well as the camera—in a more connective manner. The two women are at opposite ends of the frame, as Lucille describes her horror at seeing her father turn up by chance at the club that night. Instead of cutting between them in a traditional shot-reverse-shot, the camera pans between the young women, thus passing over the background of the sex club: we see barred windows including bits of bare bodies. As they move closer to each other, Lucille and Julie share the frame, their faces literally overcoming the windows of naked flesh on display.

By the last sequence of *Blue,* Julie's relationship to glass is physically direct. As she and Olivier make love, the camera is outside the window: we see her face right up against the glass, as if she were testing her ability to feel. There is a sense of being not only under glass but underwater, recalling Julie in the swimming pool.[5] The scene is less titillating than perturbing: even if she is reconnecting with Olivier, there is distance—not unlike their use of the formal *vous* rather than the familiar *tu* in addressing each other. The window also recalls the glass window through which her daughter is seen in the opening. In a film ostensibly about freedom, is Julie embracing her containment? By the last shot of the film, she has made peace with the window: we see her behind it,

The final lovemaking scene, *Blue*

as the blue of dawn slowly seeps into the frame from below. Tears roll down her face and she looks at what is outside the window.

This is a marked contrast to Julie's gaze earlier in *Blue*. Her injured left eye leads her to see things out-of-focus, which the subjective camera often presents. Not only are edges fuzzy, but other characters are marginalized by the frame: for example, the female reporter who asks if Julie composed her husband's music is at the edge of the screen (next to a pane of blue glass), which is where Julie—remaining in the center—wants to keep her. At the hospital, her eye reflects the doctor who tells her about the death of her family: the blinking eye merely mirrors, too numb to literally ex-press with tears. (For this shot, added after the screenplay, Kieslowski used a new 200mm lens.) By the last scene with Olivier—where an eye reflects a naked back—her tears suggest a return to life.[6]

Julie's "sight," especially inner, is expressed by Preisner's score.

The four blackouts that correspond to her consciousness—time stands still for a few beats—are accompanied by the music, uncontrollable pulsations of the past. These are sections of the *Concerto for Europe,* which her husband was commissioned to compose for the unification of the continent. We first hear the *Concerto* when Julie watches the funeral—the very melody that Preisner composed for *No End* (initially heard at a cemetery). We then "see" it when Julie retrieves the score from the copyist and throws the rolled-up sheets in a garbage truck; this is an act of self-destruction because Julie—like the score—needs to be opened in order to live. The music then returns in fragments, until she learns that Olivier has a copy and she decides to complete the *Concerto* with him. We are never certain whether Julie might have been the primary composer of her husband's music, although Kieslowski remarked that she functioned as a collaborating editor.[7]

Music has a ghostly presence in *Blue,* beginning with the scene of Julie's recuperation on the terrace of her hospital room. Her closed eyes suddenly snap open as the film's first non-diegetic music is heard: notes from the *Concerto* engender her fearful stare at the camera, which tracks away from her, and then back toward her, as blue enters the frame. She looks as if she has seen a ghost. Other sections of the *Concerto* seem to be reincarnated in the notes played by a street musician on the Rue Mouffetard. Julie, seated in her neighborhood café, hears a gentle and familiar melody on recorder; it is precisely at this moment that a close-up of part of her cup and saucer shows a shadow passing—twice.

When she asks the bearded, ponytailed musician (Jacek Ostaszewski, who is the real flutist in Preisner's orchestra for *Blue!*) where the music comes from, he says he invents all sorts of things. Kieslowski mirrors this scene when Olivier finds Julie in the café: they both recognize the notes being played on the recorder and, after he leaves, it accompanies the close-up of the sugar cube filling with dark coffee. Once again, there are transcendent possibilities in the juxtaposition of music and poetic image. As the director said in the 1994 French TV interview, "Music notes all exist, waiting for someone to order them. That two individuals in different places

Olivier plus his reflection in piano top, *Blue*

can think of the same music is an example of what unites people."

In order to write the end of the *Concerto,* Julie gives Olivier a piece of paper—the only thing she took from the house besides the chandelier. He notes that it is "a memento" in musical terms, and she adds that Patrice wanted to invoke Van Den Budenmayer (aka Preisner!) at the end. As they discuss different notes and instruments, we hear the music (how it might sound in the "conditional" tense?) while the camera moves rapidly over the score. Julie and Olivier then work separately on the *Concerto.* When she calls to tell him she is finished and he can pick up her work, he refuses: Olivier knows that his ending is not as strong as Patrice's might have been, but it is his own. He is seen together with his reflection in the piano, an apt external-ization of his split identity: he is fulfilling Patrice's score like a dutiful shadow, but he considers himself a composer in his own right. (Benoit Régent, who plays Olivier, bears a striking resemblance to Krzysztof Piesiewicz: this results in a troublingly prescient image of the collaborator who, after the death of the man he worked with, tries to complete the master's creation. This was indeed the case with the *Heaven/Hell/Purgatory* script that they were preparing when Kieslowski died.)

An unexpected tear on Julie's face is visible when she decides to bring her music to Olivier. The ensuing love scene through glass begins one of the most moving and profound sequences in all of Kieslowski's cinema. The music—which he rightly called "solemn and grand"—seems to lead the camera from Julie's face at the window to four different locales. In a very personal "unification," the *Concerto* rises: choral voices sing from the "Epistle to the Corinthians," "though I have the gift of prophecy and understand all mysteries, if I have not love, I am nothing." In a blue-toned image, a man's hand stops a ringing alarm clock; although we assume this to be Olivier, it turns out to be Antoine, who is wearing Julie's chain and touches the cross.

The camera continues its fluid movement to the right (following Antoine's glance), encountering two reflections of Julie's mother before we see her face directly. She closes her eyes as a nurse rushes in from the back. Then, like a pendulum, the camera gently moves to the left: at the sex club, two semi-nude female dancers perform on a circular device that turns toward the left, leading to a close-up of Lucille. The camera moves to the left again where a very different kind of peep show is glimpsed: a pan from a full, naked belly to a baby's outline on a sonogram then reveals Sandrine, whose smiling face is between the large blue screen and a tiny monitor. Lying horizontally, she touches the monitor—bringing us back to the early shot of Julie in the hospital, her finger on the miniature TV screen that holds the coffin of her dead child.[8]

The camera follows Sandrine's glance and shifts to the right, where an eye reflects a naked back, and then moves right to a close-up of Julie. The camera has come full circle, while incorporating the resonant circularity of Antoine's alarm clock, the sex club's turnstile, Sandrine's round belly, and the baby curled in her womb. Since the sequence begins and ends with Julie, it seems as if all these people are now part of her. The music engenders what could be called an epiphany: as the camera embraces the characters, it equalizes, forgives, and suggests hope. Whereas she had said to Olivier at the beginning, "They took everything"—referring to the furniture, but summing up her life at this stage—the last shot goes against a sense of dispossession.⁹ Julie is behind the window as if there were nothing in the world but her tears; gradually the screen fills with reflections of the outer world in which she exists. There is genuine closure as the film ends: she has completed the *Concerto* and fulfilled the mourning.

Blue can be seen as a companion piece that develops and revises aspects of *No End,* Kieslowski's first collaboration with Piesiewicz as well as Preisner. Both films begin with the death of a publically and privately beloved man; the despairing wife attempts suicide; a car crashes in the middle of *No End* and at the beginning of *Blue* (perhaps recalling the accidental death of Kieslowski's mother). Both end at a window, a threshold not only between viewer and screen but between life and death. Whereas Urszula recedes from the window, having succumbed to the lure of joining her husband's ghost, Julie remains at the glass, her eyes open. (The screenplay says she is "crying helplessly," but Kieslowski chose a more restrained and effective silent tear.) Having tried to live in "liberty"—without memory, desire, work, or commitment—she is ironically returning to love, which Kieslowski acknowledged to be contradictory with freedom. *Blue* thus reflects the refusal of pessimism articulated by Piesiewicz: "The most important things are people's dreams and their sufferings," he proposed, while acknowledging how contagious Kieslowski's pessimism can be. "That's why I want to make films which are ever more clear, to fight against this growing feeling—in myself, initially, and then in the viewer."¹⁰

Montage seems to be Kieslowski's way of achieving this ever greater clarity. Jacques Witta—the editor of *Blue* and *Red*—acknowledged at the 1997 Paris colloquium, "For 'Blue' we made thirty versions with different constructions. The film kept transforming and progressing." It certainly grew shorter, replacing exposition with economical ellipsis. If, for example, the script develops how Julie makes up a number for the lawyer—instructing him to arbitrarily put all the family money into the bank account of a person they don't know[11]—the film simply has her saying the number: its origin remains a mystery. It was indeed during the editing stage that Kieslowski became a true "composer"—arranging and rearranging the strips of celluloid like the musical notes that he said "all exist, waiting for someone to order them."

CHAPTER SEVEN

Three Colors: White

THE SECOND part of the trilogy is one of Kieslowski's deceptively simplest films, a cinematic poem—co-written by Piesiewicz—whose layered richness requires more than one viewing. *White,* which won the Best Director Prize at the 1994 Berlin Film Festival, corresponds to equality, but in the ironic sense of "getting even," or revenge. Of all three films, it is the lightest and most humorous because of its picaresque quality; nevertheless, the tone is that of very dark comedy. Editing once again proved to be the crucial stage: as with *Blue,* the final shape of *White* emerged after Kieslowski and the editor Urszula Lesiak made different versions. During the 1997 Paris colloquium, she recalled thirteen, and mentioned that the last one barely resembled the script! As Kieslowski confessed in *Variety* in 1994, "I make movies just so that I can edit them."[1]

Karol Karol (Zbigniew Zamachowski)—whose name literally means Charlie Charlie—loses everthing in a Paris courtroom: his French wife Dominique (Julie Delpy) divorces him for not consummating their marriage. The hapless hairdresser—now bereft of home, beauty salon (which they shared), car, and credit cards—is befriended in the metro by a fellow Pole,

Mikolaj (Janusz Gajos); the latter, well-to-do and world-weary, agrees to smuggle Karol back to Poland in a trunk.

Upon arriving in Warsaw, the oversized valise is stolen, and Karol emerges from it to find angry thieves; they beat him and throw him in a garbage heap from which he glimpses "home, at last." His brother Jurek (Jerzy Stuhr) is delighted to have him back, but Karol is not content to remain in their hair salon. In the newly capitalist Poland, he cleverly scrambles to entrepreneurial success, aided by Mikolaj. His aim—to get Dominique back, and to get back at Dominique—is realized when he stages his own death. She arrives for the funeral, only to be visited by a very live—and sexually potent—Karol. The long-delayed consummation of their marriage is followed by his disappearance and her arrest for his "murder." The film ends with Karol secretly visiting her in prison: each is now clearly in love with the other but trapped in his scheme.

Kieslowski tells his engaging story through recurring images, both visual and aural, beginning with the title. White is the color of an innocence that characterizes our hero at the film's opening: for example, when the judge grants Dominique the divorce, Karol throws up into a very white toilet bowl and then sits on the bathroom floor, framed between the toilet seat and a white cigarette receptacle. Even in Poland, white is virgin ice when he runs elatedly on a frozen pond with Mikolaj, who says he feels like a child again. (Karol has just fired a blank at Mikolaj: given that the French title of the film is *Blanc,* how pungent that *tirer à blanc* means firing a blank as well as shooting white! Moreover, "firing a blank" can also mean being sterile.)

From the beginning of the film, white is associated with the flapping and cooing of birds on the soundtrack, especially pigeons. A slow-motion flashback to the wedding of Karol and Dominique shows, presumably from the groom's point of view, her white veil fluttering (like wings) as they approach the church door where pigeons are cooing. We hear the same sound when he later sees the bust of a woman in a window, white like Dominique's alabaster skin; it is repeated when Karol cries out her name at night with the statue—which he has stolen—in the foreground. (This icon of female beauty is smashed by the airport thieves, but Karol lovingly puts it back together again—as he will do with his image of Dominique.) The sound of the bird returns with the flashback of the veil, and then the screen goes to white after Karol and Dominique kiss in front of the pigeons. The use of white—the color of unconsummated marriage—is particularly ironic when Dominique finally has an orgasm with Karol and the screen goes to a white-out during her screams of pleasure. By the end, she is a caged bird.

But in the present tense of the film, the first thing a pigeon does is defecate on Karol—leaving a white trace on his coat—comically foreshadowing his imminent victimization in the Paris courtroom. When we later see a bird—quite incongruously—in the metro, or flying in the warehouse where Karol buys a Russian corpse, the humor is dark indeed. Kieslowski's particularly Polish sensibility balances irony and affection for a character moving into capitalist experience (as in his *Decalogue, 10,* where Zamachowski and Stuhr play brothers trying to make a fortune from their dead father's stamp collection).

Stuart Klawans's perceptive review in *The Nation* of *Three Colors: Red* adds to an understanding of Kieslowski's imagery; he describes how at the start of *White,* "its color literally falls out of the sky onto the protagonist . . . in the form of a pigeon dropping; and from there on, Karol keeps getting whited out in emphatically material fashion, whether on the snowy streets of Warsaw or between the sheets with his estranged wife."[2] One could say that he is definitively whited out when he stages his own death; however, Karol is paradoxically making his mark.

Kieslowski's ironic tone is equally present in, and a product of, other cinematic elements, including music, casting and direction of actors, and visual style. Broke and homeless in the Paris metro, Karol plays on his comb "The Last Sunday," a popular Polish song about doomed lovers; the melody is what draws Mikolaj to him. After they get spacious new offices in

Poland, Karol plays the song on a comb again, reminding Mikolaj how far they have come. (A mere year has transpired, given that Karol returned to Poland just after Christmas, and Mikolaj is seen with Christmas gifts for the family when Karol asks him to be his business partner.)

In a larger sense, the original score by Zbigniew Preisner is narrative rather than ornamental. Whereas he composed a symphony for *Blue* and a bolero for *Red,* he created a tango for *White.* This Argentine musical form is appropriate to Kieslowski's pattern: the tango is simultaneously lyrical, playful, and deliberate—like Karol's scheme. The tango music begins after Karol has returned to Poland, and it accompanies his intricate planning. As anyone who has ever essayed an Argentine tango knows, the man is in control: even if the high-heeled, swirling-skirted woman is the one who does the flashy steps, she can move only to the extent that the man's hand—quietly but insistently controlling the bottom center of her back—allows her to. As Karol becomes increasingly self-confident via his wealth, he manipulates Dominique in an elaborate—if long-distance—dance. And, like *White,* the tango expresses romantic longing through formal constraints. (The yearning is also heard in a recurring solo, whether on oboe or clarinet.)

Kieslowski's casting and direction of actors are as supple as the tango form. Zamachowski's Karol, true to his name, is a Chaplinesque figure who strikes back resourcefully: he is introduced by a close-up of his weathered shoes before the camera tilts up to reveal this diminutive and disenfranchised outsider.[3] Delpy's Dominique, in contrast, is a dream goddess, her long golden locks a magnet to Karol's eyes and fingers. (Delpy's fair skin is beautifully photographed by Edward Klosinski, whose credits range from Andrzej Wajda's *Man of Marble* and Krzysztof Zanussi's *Camouflage* to *Decalogue, 2.*) She is certainly in charge on French soil: coldly remote in the courtroom, she then reveals a fierce vengefulness when Karol won't leave her salon. What kind of woman sets fire to her business in order to threaten her ex-husband into leaving? But once in Poland,

Dominique is as vulnerable as Karol was in France. (When the Polish policeman enters her hotel room, he asks, "Dominique Vidal?" On page 189 of the published screenplay, her name was Dominique Insdorf!)

The visual style of *White* is as playful as Preisner's tango. The opening credits are over a trunk on an airport conveyor belt—a mysterious image which will turn out to be the way that Karol is smuggled, passport-less, from Paris to Poland. As in *Blue,* sound precedes an image of mechanical movement into the heart of the frame. Since we then cut to Karol's feet approaching the Paris courthouse—presumably the film's present tense—the trunk seems to be a flash-forward. Kieslowski said in the 1994 French TV interview that he added the trunk during editing to replace something that wasn't working. "I trust the spectator to watch attentively," he added, given that the trunk creates "anticipation." Indeed, the screenplay introduction is more loud and linear:

> A wild crowd outside the department stores in the city centre. A terrible noise, vendors shouting, street organs grinding, children crying. Hell. The camera observes this sea of faces slightly from above. Slowly it distinguishes Karol from among the crowd. He approaches closer, cranes his neck and, using the camera as a mirror, scrutinizes himself. (p. 103)

Just as *Blue* pared down the screenplay indication,

> A crowded motorway. Eight lanes of cars speeding in both directions. The rumble of lorries, roar of engines, drone of motorbikes as they weave their way among the cars. Hell. (p. 3)

to one tire speeding on a highway, so *White* became more compact and elliptical. (The word "Hell" returns in the script introduction of *Red,* whose opening is identical to the screenplay. But the film's visual vibrancy hardly feels hellish.)

Kieslowski crosscuts between the trunk and the street, creating a dual axis of vision: as the camera tracks right with Karol's feet, the juxtaposition with the conveyor belt suggests that he, like the trunk, is being pulled along a predetermined path. The flash-forward is later used again in brief shots of Dominique entering a hotel room while we hear Karol's breathing: these prefigure her arrival in Warsaw. Flash-forwards embody a predestined universe; the future is already "printed" on film, so things cannot but transpire as they do.

This sense is equally true for *White* if one reads the opening image of the conveyor belt as the present tense, and Paris as the flashback. In either case, the director is playing with time: since we are not certain whether the tense is present, past, or future, he invokes the conditional tense—what might have been, or might be. Indeed, perhaps the flashback to the wedding veil is really a flash-forward, or the fantasy of an idealized future. Since this image is first presented in the courtroom after a close-up of Karol, we might assume the wedding scene is unfolding in his mind; moreover, the point of view down the aisle seems to be his, as the camera follows Dominique. But the next shot is of Dominique lost in thought, not hearing the judge's question: isn't this wedding image consequently hers?

During the last encounter between Karol and Dominique in Paris, she finds him asleep in her hair salon. He kisses her, they become aroused, he tries to penetrate her, and—once again—fails. Dominique's frustration is extreme: to get rid of him, she sets fire to the curtains, intending to tell the police that he is the arsonist. That she feels contempt for her ex-husband is underscored by the poster of Brigitte Bardot that Mikolaj glimpses when Karol points out to him where Dominique lives: mistaking the image of Bardot in Godard's *Contempt* for Dominique's window, Mikolaj says with dry humor, "Isn't she a bit over the hill?" When they finally focus on her apartment, Dominique is obviously with another man. (The *Contempt* poster is more appropriate to the moment than the script indication of Michelle Pfeiffer.)

The understated irony typical of Kieslowski continues with public telephones. The one from which Karol calls Dominique while she is having sex steals his last French coin. In Poland, injury is added to insult: the phone doesn't work, and the glass doors won't open to let Karol out. On the one hand, you can't make a simple phone call in Warsaw. On the other hand, as Mikolaj puts it, "everything is possible." As the director remarked about his country in the Miramax pressbook:

> The political and economic upheavals taking place in Poland, the result of years spent under an ultimately rejected system, had created a picturesque and photogenic muddle. It's possible to buy anything in Warsaw today: a tank, a kilo of uranium, houses whose owners have disappeared, forged passports, stolen cars, a birth certificate, a real or fake university diploma. This is the world in which our simple story unfolds.

It is a world in which religion has little function. Despite the traditional importance of the church in Poland, *White* shows it as "useful" only in two senses: when Karol has succeeded in outwitting the gangsters for whom he works, he combs his hair in the reflection from a religious painting; and when the gangsters realize they have been duped and try to kill him, Karol foils them with the declaration that his will leaves everything to the church. They are forced to buy back from him the land he purchased.

Kieslowski's irony includes the fact that Karol returns to Poland, the opposite of his fellow Eastern Europeans leaving for the West. As the director put it:

> In Poland we say, "Everyone wants to be more equal than everyone else." It's practically a proverb. And it shows that equality is impossible: it's contradictory to human nature. Hence, the failure of Communism. But it's a pretty word, and every effort must be made to help bring equality about . . . keeping in mind that we won't achieve it.[4]

Equality may be impossible, but Kieslowski does impose artistic balance on a chaotic world. For example, he gives Karol what could be called two "angels"—a paternal one in Mikolaj and a maternal one in Jurek. If the former resists emotion and is usually seen under the protective layer of a dark coat, the latter is always indoors—doing women's hair, caring for the home, or baking a loaf at the end for his brother to bring Dominique in prison. Both watch over Karol, suggesting Kieslowski's belief in a higher spirit that inheres in individuals as well as objects. When Karol tries to throw away the two-franc coin that is his last connection to France, it sticks to his palm with what could be seen as metaphysical glue. When the hidden Karol sees Dominique through binoculars crying at his funeral, Kieslowski alternates a close-up of his surprised face behind the opera glasses with a subjective shot of her loving tears. At the end of *White,* he once again alternates a close-up of Karol behind binoculars with a subjective shot of Dominique. In both scenes, Karol is a ghostly presence—seen by the audience but somewhat invisible within the frame—whose opera glasses create a "close-up": Dominique is both larger and closer in his mediated gaze.

Kieslowski's penchant for close-ups is part of a spiritual vision: when asked what he was trying to capture with this cinematic angle, he said, "Perhaps the soul. In any case, a truth which I myself haven't found. Maybe time that flies and can never be caught."[5] This comment illuminates the last scene, in which the camera—representing Karol's point of view in the prison courtyard—moves into a close-up of Dominique's face behind bars. The camera "removes" the bars via a zoom shot so that the image of her shifts from imprisoning to liberating. Her hands play out a little scene—no, she doesn't want to escape from prison; she will stay so that they can remarry—as tears roll down Karol's face. Kieslowski called it a happy ending because they both realize they love each other: "Would you rather for the story to finish with him in Warsaw and her in Paris, with both of them free but not in love?" he asked.[6]

A persuasive alternative reading of the last scene has been

Dominique behind prison window, *White*

Karol in the last shot of *White*

suggested by the Argentine psychiatrist and film critic Eduardo Newark. In an unpublished manuscript, he discusses

> the impossibility of revenge: in order to get even with her, Karol has to become a dead citizen, and Dominique an imprisoned one. The relationship is over. The zooming in to her cell window does not represent a real possibility of getting together. The human eye cannot zoom. The scene has a dream quality, in the sense that dreams represent wish-fulfillment. In real life they cannot reunite because he would have to "resurrect," to reveal that he didn't die. He would be jailed and she would be set free. There is no way out. You cannot "get even" with someone who did you wrong.

The "dream quality" to which Newark refers is reminiscent of the last scene in *A Short Film about Love,* where Magda sees through the telescope an image of herself being comforted by Tomek. The similarity of these mute exchanges led French critic Agnes Peck to invoke the term telepathy: at the 1997 Paris colloquium, she deduced from these endings that "Kieslowski presupposes a telepathic connection with the viewer."

Curiously enough, he added the last images after *White* was shot. In July of 1993, the producer Marin Karmitz received from Kieslowski a letter outlining an improved conclusion:

> I recently had an idea I'd like to share with you: it's about returning to the shot of Dominique in prison, close-up, which should be longer. In this new version, after the bars disappear, Dominique would signal to Karol. I'm thinking of something like the sign language of deaf-mutes, but much more understandable by the viewer. . . . Of course what counts for me is the language of signs, poetic and lyrical, not concrete information. I think this shot would make the end rise, and thus the film.[7]

Kieslowski was probably right, as the new ending introduces hope. Otherwise, *White* would have emphasized too strongly

Karol's new impotence, or an aspect that Paul Coates seized upon: "Allegorical readers may see Karol's vanishing, his life-in-death, as prefiguring that of the maker whose initials he shares, and take Kieslowski's avowal that the trilogy is his last work all the more seriously."[8] Dominique's signals, however, point to a spatial and temporal dimension beyond the prison. *ballet*

The dozens of deletions from script to final film render *White* more of a love story. Although one of the cuts is of Dominique—a flashback in the courtroom to when Karol first saw her—most are from scenes of the newly (and often absurdly) capitalist Poland. On the cutting room floor are "the Blonde" and "the tall man" (played by Grazyna Szapolowska of *A Short Film about Love* and Piotr Machalica of *Decalogue, 9*) from the gangster world, as well as Karol's frenzied attempts to stop the plan at the end. Instead of four pages of action including Karol appearing in the Warsaw hotel corridor, at the airport, and in his office before the startled secretary, Kieslowski follows a close-up of the apprehended Dominique with a return to the wedding image. Then, in an enigmatic close-up, Karol holds a comb before his eyes: the object that once defined him—whether as hairdresser or subway musician—now merely mediates his gaze. Another shot of the wedding makes us wonder again whether Dominique or Karol is envisioning the scene—or, more likely, both. The only truly regrettable deletion is the one that wittily connected *White* with *Red:* Karol helps two young Swiss men whose car is missing.

YOUNG MAN 2: Someone's pinched it. With our passports, money, everything.
KAROL: That's a hassle. Are you from France?
YOUNG MAN 2: Switzerland. But we're on our way to England.
KAROL: I can't offer you my place because I haven't got one myself. But you can doss down in my office. (pp. 166-7)

When Valentine is told by her boyfriend Michel during their opening phone conversation that his car was stolen in Poland and "some nice guy put us up in his office," he is indeed referring to Karol, while, on a secondary level, situating the time frame of *Red* just after *White*.

The context of the trilogy provides support for Kieslowski's optimism about the ending of *White*. The final sequence of *Red,* a ferry accident, reunites the major characters of all three films. Like a miniature Noah's ark, a lifeboat carries from the accident Julie and Olivier from *Blue,* a pair from *Red* as well as Karol and Dominique—who was presumably released from prison, and returned with renewed love to her ex-husband. *Red* culminates in reconciliation even if *White* ends in limbo, with Karol just as trapped as Dominique: equality indeed.

But this is perhaps the point of departure from which the relationship can finally work. If, as Kieslowski remarked during the French TV interview, "the real subject of 'White' is humiliation," Karol needs to transform himself. "From the very beginning," the director elaborated, "our hero is humiliated not only by the shit, but by the fact that he was smiling at the pigeon—happily, naively—before the shit fell." Other images suggest the humiliation rooted in impotence when an old man at a French recycling bin is unable to get the bottle up and in, Karol smiles nastily; in Warsaw, his gangster boss gives him a gun, adding that "it shoots only tear gas." Even the rolled-up hairdressing diplomas in Karol's trunk—seen upright when he plays a comb in the Paris metro—are tossed onto the tracks, much like Julie in *Blue* throwing the rolled-up *Concerto* scores into a garbage truck: both characters are attempting to free themselves from the immediate past.

Karol, who is impotent in Paris (invoking on a political level Eastern Europe's impotence in the West), must die and resurrect himself in Poland for the relationship to resume. Death and resurrection figure prominently in *White,* beginning with Mikolaj's disconcerting offer to Karol: he knows of a man who wants to kill himself but is unable to and will pay someone to shoot him. Karol accepts, arrives in the designated place (the outdoor rubbish dump in the script, changed to the the abandoned metro tracks in the film, connecting to his first meeting with Mikolaj), and finds that the suicidal target is none other than Mikolaj—who pays him and insists that he fulfill the mission. Karol shoots him. But he has used a blank, and when Mikolaj opens his eyes, Karol asks if he is sure that he still wants to go through with it. Having almost died is enough: the two go out drinking instead.

Karol, too, stages his own death; but as with Mikolaj, it is deceptive, and death turns out not to be the answer. Both "die" to be reborn, getting a second chance (a theme that permeates the trilogy). Karol and Dominique, for example, will get another opportunity to love each other—now that they are "equal" after mutual emotional violence. In this regard, the symmetry of the director's images—including variations on white, pigeons, the male gaze, song-on-comb, telephones, and faked death—nourishes the notion of second chances: repetition becomes accumulation, with a prior mistake as a base for successful action.

At the beginning, Karol stares up at Dominique's Paris window; unable to bear the sight of a man's silhouette next to hers, he phones her hysterically (reminiscent of Tomek in *A Short Film about Love*). At the end, he stares up silently at her window in the Warsaw prison. The second time, Dominique returns his gaze—and with love. Having overcome language barriers, their communication is wordless. Separated in space, they are nevertheless united by Kieslowski's expressive technique—a poetic blend of camera placement and movement, sound and music, editing and vision.

CHAPTER EIGHT

Three Colors: *Red*

IF FRATERNITY can be defined as being close to one's neighbors, *Red* is certainly about fraternal ties: in Kieslowski's ironic twist, a retired Judge (Jean-Louis Trintignant) secretly listens in to his neighbors' phone conversations. But the deeper exploration of *Red* concerns the growing bond between the crusty Judge and Valentine (Irene Jacob), a radiant model and student at the University of Geneva. Is friendship possible between a man and a woman in today's world? Perhaps, at least in the profoundly humanist tale written by Kieslowski and Piesiewicz.

The cinematography by Piotr Sobocinski (who shot *Decalogue, 3* and *9* and went on to success in the United States as the director of photography for Ron Howard's *Ransom* and Robert Benton's *Twilight*) is an integral part of the story, as *Red* is structured through internal rhymes and haunting parallels. Less a linear construction than an intricate play of reflections, the third part of the trilogy is punctuated by recurring images—including telephones, cars, flashing lights, and splashes of red—that suggest the desire for contact as well as the fear of intimacy. Preisner's "bolero" is a brilliant aural complement: the lyrical melodic theme is developed and then repeated, its very structure expressing the cumulative resonance characteristic of *Red*.

From the outset of the film, Valentine and her neighbor Auguste (Jean-Pierre Lorit) almost meet—but not quite—even though the camera constantly connects them for the audience. Warm and open, Valentine struggles with a long-distance boyfriend who exists only as a jealous voice on her phone. Auguste, romantically involved with Karin (Frédérique Feder), is about to take the exam that will render him a judge. When Valentine accidentally runs over a dog, she places the injured animal Rita in her car and drives her to the owner, the retired Judge. But he is indifferent, and Valentine cares for the dog herself.

When healed, Rita runs back to her master's house, leading Valentine to follow: she is shocked and angered to discover what has been plainly left for her to see—the Judge's surveillance equipment. This encounter leaves her in tears and prompts the Judge to write letters denouncing himself to his wronged neighbors as well as the police.

Although he is not named in the film's closing credits, the Judge shows up at court as defendant and we hear the case announced as "the people vs. Joseph Kern" (rendering more than coincidental that the neighborhood café of Valentine and Auguste is "Chez Joseph"). When Valentine reads about this local privacy-invasion scandal in the newspaper, she rushes to the Judge's home to tell him she did not betray his secret. Like Alexandre in *The Double Life of Veronique,* he replies that he denounced himself to see what she would do. Their ensuing conversation is a true rapprochement, a bonding during which he encourages her to take the ferry for her upcoming trip to England. Is he aware that Auguste will take the same ferry from listening in on his phone calls? He clearly does know that Karin—who has fallen for another man—will be on the same waters in the new lover's yacht. Auguste has passed the jurisprudence exam but has failed in his romance. (When he furtively climbs up to Karin's window and sees her in a naked embrace, he puts himself in the same position as Tomek in *A Short Film about Love,* Roman in *Decalogue, 9,* and Karol in *White*—peep-ing on what he most fears.)

The Judge accepts Valentine's invitation to a fashion show in which she models, and they speak frankly in the abandoned theater afterward. Whereas he had been the one who was aware of everyone's stories, she now divines his own. As Valentine recounts his past, the parallels to Auguste's present are unmistakable: the Judge too was betrayed by a blonde woman two years older than him. Like his young double Auguste (in an earlier scene), his book fell open to a particular page before his exam—and he was asked the very question found on that page. "Maybe you're the woman I never met," the Judge says quietly to Valentine.

Auguste will finally meet her in the film's last scene: as the Judge watches the news on a television screen, the survivors of a massive ferry accident emerge, ending with Auguste and then

Valentine and Auguste at the end of *Red*

Valentine in the same frame. The other survivors include Julie and Olivier from *Blue,* as well as Karol and Dominique from *White.* The trilogy comes full circle within one year: the TV announcer's voice mentions that Julie's husband died a year ago.

The opening credit sequence of *Red* is consistent with the first two segments of the trilogy, setting up the film thematically and stylistically. Sound precedes image as we once again hear a rumbling that will turn out to be mechanical: after the car wheel of *Blue* and the conveyor belt of *White,* the whirring in *Red* is related to a man's hand dialing a phone. (A second viewing makes clear that the photo by the telephone is of Valentine, and the caller is her boyfriend Michel. The sound includes rain, presaging Michel's comment, "Typical English weather. It's pouring.") The camera's exhilarating physical trajectory begins with a whip pan to the left, following the phone wire, and then enters the filaments: it zips underwater, as we hear distorted voices and sounds, conveying the technological path that the human spirit must travel in the 1990s. Circular lights flash with the sound of beeping: the line is busy. The call is placed again, and contact is made. "Redial" could serve as the subtitle of Kieslowski's oeuvre. The story of *Red* gives the character of the aged Judge a second chance via Valentine to be human; at the end of the trilogy, she too is given a second chance—whether by fate, God, or the Judge-as-magician—to escape the ferry crash and be "reborn" together with a younger version of the Judge.

The opening of *Red* introduces numerous elements, from the phone (or surveillance) to the omniscient camera, and from crossed wires (or missed connections) to chance. For the Judge, telephones exist like radio, to be listened to rather than spoken on. He and Valentine never call each other; rather, she comes in person to see him, or he makes the trip to her fashion show after receiving a written invitation. For Auguste, who doesn't have an answering machine, the phone is problematic: he misses Karin's call at a crucial moment and gets a busy signal when he then tries to reach her. Karin lives by the phone, having created a personalized weather service: people who are about to take a trip call to get information about their destination. And for Valentine, the phone is a source of frustration: each time Michel calls, he berates her for not having answered a previous time. Indeed, this jealous boyfriend seems to be spying on her, sensing that she could have picked up the phone earlier.

However, given that the audience's entry into *Red* is through overhearing the unseen boyfriend's conversation with Valentine, our relationship to Michel is like the Judge's to everyone—eavesdroppers. And we are hardly alone: when the Judge dares Valentine to go next door and tell a married man (who is on the phone with his male lover) that the Judge hears them, she goes, only to find that the man's daughter is secretly listening to her father's conversation on an extension.

The camera's elegant but deliberate movements suggest a benign surveillance as well. Like the Judge, the camera seems to be aware of everyone simultaneously. For example, even before Valentine picks up the phone, the camera introduces Auguste in his apartment. He too makes a call—earlier than in the script—consisting of a quick and enigmatic kiss. A ringing phone leads the camera out of his place—past the red awning of the café "Chez Joseph"—and into the window of Valentine's apartment. The camera waits for the protagonist: we hear her voice on the answering machine while the movement of a red rocking chair suggests her vibrating presence. (When she rushes into the frame to pick up the phone, the audience is as relieved as the caller.) The camera has an omniscient life of its own, as when it tracks back to the Judge after Valentine leaves his house. At a bowling alley, it not only follows a bowling ball about to knock down the pins but tracks left from Valentine to a broken glass and crumpled pack of Marlboros. Given that the Marlboro-smoking Auguste was supposed to meet Karin at the bowling alley, the camera indirectly tells us she never showed up. (The broken glass at the bowling alley also connects visually to the cracked plastic coffee cup in Valentine's hand during her final interchange with the Judge.) When the Judge describes to Valentine how he wrote letters to all his telephonic objects, the camera tracks left again—breathlessly, self-consciously, and ambiguously—to glass jars in another room before returning. And in their last encounter at the theater, when the Judge recounts to Valentine that his book fell open from the balcony—onto a page containing the question that would appear on his exam—a camera tilt viscerally mimics the fall of the book.[1]

Was it chance that the text opened to this page? And is it chance that Auguste's book falls open in the same way—indeed to a page containing the question he will be asked? In Kieslowski's poetic universe of convergences, probably not. Valentine wonders to Michel whether they would have ever met had she not stepped out for a break. Later, she stops in to the café for her daily ritual of playing the slot machine. And when the Judge makes her listen to a conversation between Auguste and Karin, the question of whether they will go bowling is resolved by a coin: Karin and the Judge toss at the same time, both getting tails. The Judge's subtle smile suggests that chance is merely the mask of destiny.

The camera's intricate choreography, combined with the use of red, presents a world in which little has been left to chance. "Retroactive reasoning" is the term Kieslowski invoked to describe the enhanced repetition of images: as Sobocinski put it,

> There was no storyboard of course, just associations whose meanings must be hidden rather than disclosed. . . . Having then defined a network of subtle associations, we reversed the usual cinematic logic. Instead of omens forewarning of some future happening, we designed later scenes to show that some earlier, apparently casual events, were important to the story.[2]

For example, the circular flashing bulbs of the opening set up the notion of light as movement, which is developed throughout *Red*. When Valentine's parked car emits alarm sounds, she sees the headlights flashing from her window. And when

Auguste, distraught after witnessing Karin's sexual betrayal, leaves his red jeep under Valentine's window, she notices that the battery will soon die out. During her second visit to the Judge, he pauses in mid-conversation to alert her to the light: it is about to glow through the room. And during her third visit, they converse through twilight until he turns on a table lamp. The bulb doesn't work. He puts in another, which emits a harsh glare until he places the shade over it.

In an unpublished paper, Barnard College student Joanna Present likens the Judge's house to a camera: "Light comes through it at a known angle and point in time." The heightened awareness of light—both the Judge's and Kieslowski's—does not merely make us aware of watching a film; it also questions where illumination comes from, literally and figuratively. As in Bernardo Bertolucci's *The Conformist*—which starred Trintignant as the confused fascist assassin Marcello in 1930s Italy—lucidity is a function of light: what we see depends on how it is illuminated, like the professor graphically embodying Plato's "Myth of the Cave" to Marcello by opening a window and erasing shadows. (It is no coincidence that Sobocinski claimed Vittorio Storaro, cinematographer of *The Conformist,* as a major influence on his work.)

Both *Red* and *The Conformist* use the self-conscious repetition of images and colors to connect two periods in time. Here, the bitter past of the Judge is invoked as a frame for the turbulent present of Auguste—even if we realize this connection only toward the end of the film. As Janet Maslin wrote about *Red* in her laudatory review, "Stories develop like photographs in a darkroom. They are sharply defined only in retrospect, when the process is complete."[3] It is only on second viewing that the viewer recognizes how the very color red has connected characters, scenes, and perhaps temporal dimensions. As soon as Auguste goes into the street with his dog, a red car almost hits the animal. The red cherries on Valentine's yogurt label when she answers Michel's call are picked up when she plays the slot machine in the café; the red ribbon on her TV antenna relates not only to the red sweater she will later wear but to Auguste's shirt. She tells Michel that she missed him and slept in his jacket: its red prepares for the billboard background of her chewing gum ad. The dog's blood on her hands connects with her red leash, as well as with the walls of the veterinarian's office, the headlights of her car at night, and her bowling ball. The seats are red in the bowling alley, as are the seats in the theater where the fashion show takes place. The ferry ticket is as red as the wrapper of the bottle of pear liqueur that the Judge gives Valentine as a parting gift.

Why the predominance of this color? At the beginning, the flashing red light means "stop": the phone call can't go further because the line is busy. If red also signals "stop" at the traffic light, we can surmise that the color means interdiction. Indeed, the Judge must stop spying on his neighbors, and Valentine can't go on taking her boyfriend's jealous scenes. In this light, the end of the film takes on even more resonance: freeze-frames literally arrest the characters in motion, perhaps foreshadowing Kieslowski himself—about to stop directing.

Irene Jacob offered a provocative response in the press kit—prepared by Miramax for the American release—when she said that her character and the Judge "blush inside themselves, red for rage, shame and confusion." Red suggests the pulsating of blood in the body—not necessarily violent or sexual, as in other films, but a rhythm like that of telephone wires that physically transport the human spirit. Brown—the derivative of red that Sobocinski visualized as the film's dominant color—is part of this associative fabric. For example, the first shot of Auguste's apartment includes a brown-toned painting of a female ballet dancer. This idealized image of female beauty in motion will be "incarnated" when Valentine arches her back in the same position during ballet class. Similarly, the inflated image of Valentine's red-toned billboard presents her left profile in precisely the same manner that the TV screen will show her face after the ferry accident (with something reddish-brown behind her); the gray sweater on her shoulders foreshadows the gray blanket around her neck after she is rescued. In Kieslowski's words, "Fate was pre-ordained: the image of her existed before the catastrophe. Maybe there is fate, an image that has to repeat itself. It's more a Greek than religious concept."[4]

The image repeats itself even within Kieslowski's frames: when Valentine comes to the Judge's house, she is reflected in two mirrors; on her second visit, she is again reflected in his glass frame. This visual layering is particularly striking after the first fashion show when a tired Valentine is seated behind the wheel of her car: the camera is not only outside the windshield—containing reflected lights—but positioned behind the revolving glass door of the hotel. This creates the feeling that someone is watching her, even if her image is too complex to seize. Is she already the Judge's target?

It is at this point that Valentine drives home, hitting Rita just past the highway intersection. She has been fiddling with the car radio, whose distorting sound waves are interrupting the beautiful melody (Preisner's theme, introduced at the fashion show, but now presented diegetically). The radio distracts her from the road, leading her to run over the dog. Since sound is the Judge's domain in *Red,* in retrospect his presence hovers over the scene.

His association with music continues in a subtle but mischievous way. He leaves the money for Valentine's veterinarian on top of an album cover: when Valentine picks it up, we glimpse an image of a man in powdered wig and the letters "mayer." Later, in a record store she listens on headphones to the music of Van Den Budenmayer while, just across the aisle, Auguste and Karin are appreciating the same CD. She tries to buy it, but they have just purchased the last copy. On the CD jacket is the same picture as the album in the Judge's home. (For those familiar with *Decalogue, 9,* this is the very music that the young woman Ola sang before her heart operation. And as if these eye-winking references weren't enough, the astute viewer can catch a few notes of Preisner's tango from *White* as Valentine leaves the record store.)

It is no surprise that both the Judge and Auguste are fans of Van Den Budenmayer; after all, each wears suspenders and has a dog, too. Their doubling is occasionally ironic: at the same time that Karin gives Auguste a new pen, the Judge has to use a pencil to write self-denunciating letters because no ink is left in his pen. This image of impotence can be connected to the fact that his car battery is dead (he gets a new one to drive to Valentine's fashion show), that he walks with a cane, and that he purposely spills water from a teapot onto the floor when Valentine refuses tea: in Stuart Klawans's astute opinion, "What a flaunting of desire, with what an avowal of impotence! What haughtiness, combined with what ramshackle despair!"[5] An aural voyeur, the Judge can only spy and manipulate indirectly.

The Judge's presence is so mysteriously palpable throughout *Red* that one can ask whether Auguste has any real existence of his own or is merely an echo of the Judge. Ultimately, they are reflections of each other, for as Kieslowski put it:

> The theme of "Red" is in the conditional mood . . . what would have happened if the Judge had been born forty years later. . . . It would be lovely if we could go back to the age of twenty. How many better, wiser things we could have done! But it's impossible. That's why I made this film—that maybe life can be lived better than we do.[6]

There is indeed a compensatory vision throughout *Red:* if Valentine counts six rocks that have been hurled by neighbors through the Judge's window, six survivors of the trilogy are rescued at the end. (Rita, who might have died, gives birth to seven puppies, the total number of survivors.)[7] When Valentine wins coins at the café slot machine, it is to compensate for seeing her brother's picture (as a drug addict) in the newspaper. A

The judge at the end of *Red*

shot of three cherries on this machine is intercut when Auguste dashes to find Karin in a compromising position: we guess he is about to lose something. The sexual betrayal he witnesses connects him not only to the Judge, but to the rest of the trilogy: in *Blue*, Julie learns that her husband had a mistress; in *White*, Dominique flaunts a lover to Karol when he phones her. But Julie redeems the situation by offering the mistress the family home and name, and Dominique seems to choose solitude and love for Karol over freedom without him.[8]

The last shots of all three films present the hard-won victories of the characters over isolation and despair. A window is prominent in each: like Julie behind the glass of *Blue* and Dominique looking out the barred window of *White*, the Judge is seen through his broken window (which is absent from the screenplay). The tear on his face reveals a person capable of finally crying—much like Julie and Karol at the end of the previous two films. Before Kieslowski rescues all these characters from the ferry accident, they essentially save themselves. A stylistic detail connects the end of the trilogy to the beginning of *The Decalogue,* underlining the unity of Kieslowski's cinematic universe. The still of Valentine on the TV screen recalls the freeze-frame of little Pavel in *Decalogue, 1*—the ghostly presence of another accident victim.

That the Judge is a double not only for Auguste but for Kieslowski can be surmised from a number of haunting connections that include Shakespeare's *Tempest.* If the director acknowledged during a private conversation in 1994, "I learned that my neighbor had been listening to my phone conversations," he later admitted wryly. "Of course, I peep and eavesdrop on my characters—but not in life." As with *The Tempest,* not only was *Red* the artist's last work, but the central male character reflects aspects of the artists. Prospero and the Judge are old men who have lived in isolation, nursing grudges and giving up on humanity.

Each makes a decisive break with misanthropy because of a beautiful young woman.[9] In Shakespeare's masterpiece, it is Prospero's daughter Miranda who is released from the island in order to love the young man Prospero has brought to her. In Kieslowski's final work, the catharsis is wrought by the somewhat filial Valentine, whose first interchange with the Judge establishes a charged subtext: when he doesn't seem to care that his dog is injured, she asks, "If I ran over your daughter, would you be so indifferent?" "I have no daughter, miss," he replies coolly. Given that Valentine's father is conspicuous in his absence, this conversation suggests the roles they might end up playing for each other.

Like Prospero, the Judge seems to have prophetic powers. His uncanny knowledge of Valentine's thoughts led Anthony Lane to propose in *The New Yorker* an intriguing connection to *The Silence of the Lambs:* "Like Hannibal Lecter without the appetite, he cross-examines Valentine as if she, and not he, had committed a crime, guessing her family problems—her brother is a junkie—and predicting her future."[10] But if Shakespeare's magician actually creates a storm, the one that causes the ferry accident of *Red* cannot be traced directly to Kieslowski's enigmatic cynic. The Judge must watch the TV to learn what happened to his neighbors on the turbulent seas. Kieslowski likened the Judge to "a director" who allows

> the trilogy to begin. . . . For me he resembles a chess-player who foresees the movements of the game. . . . Does the Judge even exist? To be honest, the only proof . . . is the tribunal, the sole place where we see him with other people. Otherwise he could be merely a ghost, or better yet, a possibility—the old age that awaits Auguste, what might have happened if Auguste had not taken the ferry.[11]

Kieslowski once quipped that *Red* is a film about the weather, unaware of how appropriate the English homonym is: *Red* is a film about the "whether." And if the telephone can be seen as the Judge's instrument, he does perhaps "raise his wand" when he finally picks up the receiver to call Karin for climate predictions. (As an audience member at the 1997 Paris colloquium pointed out, *Decalogue, 1* and *Red* are linked by a statistical prediction that turns out to be false.)

Like the setting sun noticed by Valentine, the casting of Jean-Louis Trintignant as the Judge adds another autumnal layer to *Red*. The romantic lead of earlier films like *A Man and a Woman,* this French actor also starred as an aging anti-hero in the last film of François Truffaut, *Confidentially Yours* (1983); both filmmakers died within a year after their last movies. Trintignant plays an alter ego of the director, whether co-starring with Truffaut's beloved Fanny Ardant (allowing her character to save his) or with Kieslowski's luminous Irene Jacob (who brings out in the Judge repressed feelings of compassion and hope). His renunciation of tampering with people's lives in *Red* reflects Kieslowski's "breaking of the wand" as surely as Prospero's renunciation reflected Shakespeare's.

In his thoughtful and probing essay, "To Save the World," Dave Kehr elaborates on the resonances of the Judge's character:

> Trintignant is that Old Testament God, but a pathetically diminished one, whose power extends to light bulbs but not lightning, and whose apparent control over the winds and seas may be explained by the fact that he knows a good number to call for a personalized weather forecast. He may not be a god at all, but merely a man who takes himself for one— like filmmakers do, when they create their little worlds and send their characters scurrying through them. Trintignant invests the Judge with much of Kieslowski's own flinty contrariness, and it isn't hard to imagine the solitary smoker of Kieslowski's retirement occupying a house just like the judge's, sitting just as quietly amid the clutter of a lifetime.[12]

When the film was completed, Kieslowski stated that he was exhausted and would direct no more movies after *Red:* "If I had made the films separately, I'd have lost six years of my life. So I won three years," he said wryly in Cannes about the trilogy. Was he staging his own professional death in order to be born again? Here we can recall from *White* the character of Mikolaj who has "no motivation to live." If Mikolaj is tired, the Judge is retired, and says to Valentine, "I want nothing." "Stop breathing," she replies. "Good idea," he counters. These are perhaps emblems of Kieslowski, a cynical man who is nevertheless revitalized. As Stuart Klawans wrote, "Like Prospero drowning his book, our modern-day wizard has gone out with a splash. A muted splash: Although Krzysztof Kieslowski's *Red* works up to a full-scale tempest at sea, the heart of its story lies in an old man's act of abnegation." Following Kehr's lead, he likens the Judge to Kieslowski, "who, throughout his career has used sophisticated electronic equipment . . . to track the intersection of people's lives. . . . Now, upon his retirement, his screen double appears before us in the form of a judge, who at last shuts off the eavesdropping machinery and allows life to proceed without his surveillance."[13]

At the 1997 Paris colloquium, Piesiewicz was probably invoking *Red* when he admitted about Kieslowski, "we feared him, in the best sense of the term. He was a judge, a good judge, a good frame of reference." And the director was quite frank in stating about the character of the Judge, "to a great extent, he reflects my world-view. That's why I've often said that 'Red' is very close to me." Nevertheless, he added, "There is also this naive look that Valentine casts on people and things. . . . You could say that their opposing positions are mine."[14] Irene Jacob echoed this sentiment when she wrote, "The confrontation between these two characters surely corresponds to an interior questioning for Krzysztof: how can the hopes of youth coexist with the experience of maturity?"[15]

As we approach the millennium, *Three Colors* seems like a timely work: at the end of a century riddled with mistakes, Kieslowski's characters enact an ultimately compassionate sce-

Valentine at recycling bin, *Red*

nario. The recurrence of an aged person at a recycling bin in each film questions what Tennessee Williams termed "the kindness of strangers": if Julie in *Blue* doesn't see an old woman trying to push a bottle into a recycling bin, and Karol in *White* ignores an old man struggling to do the same, Valentine assists the aged woman she notices. At the 1994 New York Film Festival, Kieslowski confessed about this scene, "All I want to say is, 'You can help an old woman who is too old to get the bottle in.' It's just a reminder that someday, we too might be too old to push a bottle into a bin." Valentine's action with this stranger is as redemptive as her concern for the Judge: like the audience, he is touched by the grace of a person who, quite simply, does good. Valentine fulfills Piesiewicz's succinct statement, " 'Red' is a film against indifference."[16]

Despite the fact that *Red* was ignored by the jury of the 1994 Cannes Film Festival—which led numerous critics and filmmakers to use the word "scandalous"—it had unprecedented success in the United States. Kehr was one of many critics who used heightened language to describe *Red:* he called the trilogy "an epic of reconciliation," and praised moments through which "Kieslowski makes it seem as if the entire work were moving toward a single point of convergence, toward one grand climax. It's the narrative equivalent of a planetary alignment."[17] Besides being voted best foreign film by the National Society of Film Critics as well as the New York Film Critics Circle, *Red* earned three Academy Award nominations—best director, best original screenplay, and best cinematography—a rare honor for foreign filmmakers.

In France, *Red* sealed Kieslowski's reputation as what Agnes Peck called "the most important European filmmaker," for which she offered three compelling reasons:

First, he is the inheritor of a central-European cultural tradition which has always blended aesthetic and intellectual reflection, by confronting the principal existential themes— of love and death, of chance and destiny. Second, he proposes a real humanism, far from moralism or ideology, which attests to a keen sense of relativity and ambiguity, and questions the audience about our times. Finally, besides the intellectual pleasure offered by this multiplicity of layers of apprehension—this psychological and moral delicacy which has nothing to envy from literature—Kieslowski's cinema procures a rare sensual pleasure.[18]

Kieslowski, of course, did not live long enough to become a stooped septuagenarian at a recycling bin. On March 13, 1996, following elective heart surgery in a Warsaw hospital, he died. Tired and retired, but still teaching at the Lodz Film School as well as Katowice, he went a step further than his characters in the trilogy: he withdrew from the visible world, leaving behind a ghostly trace.

Epilogue

Pawel: What remains after someone dies?
Krzysztof: What a man has done.
—*Decalogue, 1* —Kubrick

DURING THE last few years of Kieslowski's life, the director tended toward despairing pronouncements. Some were about the world, others about himself. In the 1994 French television interview, he said, "Film has lost its importance. In the sixties, seventies and early eighties, movies counted. Because everyone was against the Communist system, it was easy for us to tell stories the public understood, even during censorship. Now, the audience doesn't know what it wants to see, and we don't know what we want to say." He was becoming increasingly tired of the processes of filmmaking—with the notable exception of casting and editing: in the same TV program, he described screenwriting as long and monotonous, location scouting as tedious, and shooting as boring. "All I'll miss is the editing table," he concluded. Poetry

It is hard to reconcile the pleasure a viewer takes from Kieslowski's films with the director's own fatigued dismissals of artistry. For example, he told Danusia Stok, "But really I make films because I don't know how to do anything else. It was a poor choice I made in the past . . . today I know it was the wrong one. This is a very difficult profession: it's very costly, very tiring, and gives one very little satisfaction in proportion to the effort expended."[1] Gone is the exhilaration naively experienced by Filip making movies in *Camera Buff*. Rather, producer Marin Karmitz alluded to a gnawing self-consciousness in Kieslowski: "I know he considered 'Red' his best film; but then, the very serious question for him was whether he could go even further, or if he risked repeating himself. Hence the questions we can ask about his death."[2]

Kieslowski was neither overly nor overtly fond of organized religion, but his later work emanates a belief in the life of the spirit. When someone called him a "moralist" at the 1994 Cannes Film Festival, he refused the label; to the follow-up question of "metaphysician?" he shrugged and said, "if you wish." If Kieslowski still seems so present to many of us, maybe it's because of the transcendence in which he seemed to believe—his "impression that there must be more things beyond what we can see," as he put it in *I'm So-So*.

Concretely speaking, Kieslowski's legacy includes an as-yet-unfilmed trilogy, and a prize in his name for young filmmakers in France. He had begun working with Piesiewicz on the screenplays for *Heaven, Hell,* and *Purgatory*. The first script, set in Italy, was completed by Piesiewicz (who mentioned to me in August of 1998 that he was also writing the scripts for movies entitled *Faith* and *Love*). Harvey Weinstein quoted Kieslowski as having told him, "I have this idea about a trilogy on heaven, hell and purgatory, set in three different cities. I don't know yet where I'd set heaven or purgatory, but I think I'd set hell in L.A."[3]

In Paris, Marin Karmitz's production company MK2 created the annual Prix Kieslowski in 1997, open to aspiring filmmakers between sixteen and twenty-six years of age. Applicants submitted scripts of no more than five pages each on the themes of Citizenship, Respect, and Justice. MK2 financed the making of three short films based on the winning script for each theme and then exhibited the winners in its numerous movie theaters. In 1998, the contest had different themes—Giving, Receiving,

Sharing—and again awarded the Prix Kieslowski to the winning script in each category.

This prize probably would have pleased Kieslowski, who spent so much time working with film students. He taught directing and screenwriting not only at his alma mater in Lodz but at Katowice in Poland, Berlin, Helsinki, and Switzerland. At a Boston press conference in 1995, he used the metaphor, "A train is going somewhere, and the car of film is very crowded. In order for others to get on, someone has to get off to make room." But instead of making room, Krzysztof Kieslowski left a void that has not yet been filled.

CHAPTER 1. PERSONAL BACKGROUND, STUDENT FILMS,
DOCUMENTARIES

1. My conversation with Irena Strzalkowska, administrative head of the TOR film unit, Paris, May 1997.

2. Kieslowski acknowledged during his press conference for *Red* at the 1994 New York Film Festival, "There isn't money in Poland, not for film schools, and not for hospitals—which is a more serious problem."

3. My conversation with Eva Hoffman in New York, October 27, 1997.

4. Jean-Louis Trintignant interviewed by Pierre Murat, *Télérama* (hors-série, September 1993), p. 56.

5. Joan Dupont, "Film Variations in Red, White and Blue," *International Herald Tribune,* August 31, 1993.

6. Kieslowski's 1968 graduating thesis was published in *Film Na Swiecie* (Poland, 1992), no. 34. Michel Lisowski's French translation appeared in *Positif* (March 1995), no. 409, and was reprinted in *Krzysztof Kieslowski: Textes réunis et présentés par Vincent Amiel* (Paris: POSITIF/Jean-Michel Place, 1997), p. 26. Translations from the French are my own.

7. Amiel, p. 25.

8. *Kieslowski on Kieslowski,* edited by Danusia Stok (London: Faber and Faber, 1993), p. 39, and Krzysztof Krubski et al, *Filmowka: powiesc o Lodzkiej Skole Filmowej* (Warsaw: Tenten Publishing, 1993), p. 81.

9. Betsy Sherman, "Kieslowski Uncovers Poetic Mystery in the Everyday," *The Boston Sunday Globe,* January 23, 1994, p. B36.

10. Interview with Jacques Demeure, *Positif* (February 1980), no. 227, reprinted in Amiel, p. 38.

11. *Kieslowski on Kieslowski,* p. 64.

12. Interview with Hubert Niogret, *Positif* (December 1989), no. 346, reprinted in Amiel, p. 71.

13. *Kieslowski on Kieslowski,* p. 78.

CHAPTER 2. EARLY FICTION

1. From *Positif* (May 1996), no. 423, reprinted in Amiel, p. 16.

2. *Kieslowski on Kieslowski,* p. 60.

3. Ibid., pp. 96–7.

4. Ibid., p. 99. Despite his negative feeling about *The Scar,* Kieslowski also made *Slate* (*Klaps,* 1976), a 6-minute short from footage that was not used in the final cut.

5. Ibid., p. 108. This book says that the running time for "The Calm" is 44 minutes; however, the version I received from Film Polski runs 70 minutes.

6. Jean Gili, *Positif* (December 1988), no. 334, reprinted in Amiel, p. 52.

7. *Kieslowski on Kieslowski,* p. 86.

8. Ibid., p. 208.

9. Amiel, p. 40.

10. *Kieslowski on Kieslowski,* p. 59.

11. Ibid., p. 38.

12. Amiel, p. 58.

CHAPTER 3. CHANCE AND DEATH

1. Maria Kornatowska, " . . . Yet We Do Not Know What Will Become of Us": On the Artistic Output of Wojciech Jerzy

Has,"*Bulletin de la Société des Sciences et des Lettres de Lodz,* Volume VI ("Polish Cinema in Ten Takes"), Lodz, 1995, pp. 41–2.

2. Alain Masson, *Positif* (December 1988), no. 334, reprinted in Amiel, p. 57.

3. *Kieslowski on Kieslowski,* p. 127. Piesiewicz was one of the prosecuting lawyers for the family of the priest Jerzy Popieluzko—murdered in October 1984—during the famous trial against three state security officers in Torún. He was also a senator in Parliament, representing the Solidarity movement.

4. Casting Jerzy Radziwillowicz as Antek in *No End* invokes associations with the characters he incarnated for Wajda: in *Man of Marble,* he plays the socialist hero and victim Birkut; in *Man of Iron,* Radziwillowicz plays Birkut's son, the emblem of Solidarity.

5. *Kieslowski on Kieslowski,* p. 134.

6. Ibid., p. 130.

7. Ibid., p. 136.

8. Interview by Annette Insdorf, *Chicago Sun Times,* October 15, 1989.

CHAPTER 4. *THE DECALOGUE*—TEN SHORT FILMS ABOUT MORTALITY
1. Richard Corliss, "The Best of 1998," *Time Magazine* (December 21, 1998).

2. Interview by Michel Ciment, *Positif* (December 1989), no. 346, reprinted in Amiel, p. 165. Kieslowski said, "When we wonder why a person had a certain destiny, we look for the sources and discover the importance of chance. . . . It's by chance that I met Piesiewicz, without whom I would probably never have made 'The Decalogue.' Maybe it was also fate. I had to meet Piesiewicz." Interview by Michel Ciment and Hubert Niogret, *Positif* (December 1989), no. 346, reprinted in Amiel, p. 101.

3. *Kieslowski on Kieslowski,* p. 143.

4. Interview by Annette Insdorf, *The New York Times,* (October 28, 1990), "Arts and Leisure," p. 28.

5. As Kieslowski told Michel Ciment and Hubert Niogret, "Besides Sobocinski who shot two episodes, there was a different cinematographer for each film. That's the best idea I had for this 'Decalogue.' Shooting is so boring that I looked for a way to remedy it. With the arrival each time of a new director of photography, everything changed. He had different ideas for the lighting and a thousand other things." In Amiel, p. 95.

6. Insdorf, *The New York Times*.

7. Krzysztof Kieslowski and Krzysztof Piesiewicz, *Decalogue: The Ten Commandments*, translated by Phil Cavendish and Susannah Bluh (London: Faber and Faber, 1991), p. xiii.

8. René Prédal in *Etudes Cinématographiques: Krzysztof Kieslowski* (Paris: Lettres Modernes, 1994), p. 66.

10. The casting of *Decalogue, 1* was complicated. Henryk Baranowski, who is a theater director rather than an actor, told me in October 1998 that Kieslowski lost the actor who was to play the father. Kieslowski tried doing the role himself, saw that he was—in his own words—"no good," and asked Baranowski to step in. Moreover, once they began shooting, the boy originally cast as Pawel was replaced by Wojciech Klata.

11. Joel Magny in *Etudes Cinématographiques*, p. 87.

12. *Decalogue*, p. 3. Subsequent page numbers are from this edition.

13. Amiel, p. 99. A provocative interpretation was offered by French critic Veronique Campan when she compared the silent man to "the mythic figure Ahasverus, the Jew condemned to wander, excluded from every place and time, because he refused to recognize the image of the divine in Jesus." In *Dix brèves histoires d'image* (Paris: Presses de la Sorbonne Nouvelle, 1993), p. 51. Delmore

14. *Kieslowski on Kieslowski*, p. 149.

15. Although *Decalogue, 1* never explains the mother's absence—she is seven hours away in time-zone terms, suggesting Chicago—Kieslowski subtly indicates that the parents are estranged: Krzysztof does not hide from Pawel that he is going out on a date, dabbing cologne under his ears.

16. Amiel, p. 84.

17. Ibid., p. 100.

18. Ibid., p. 85.

19. *Decalogue, 2* is invoked in *5* aurally as well: when the driver turns on the car radio, the announcer says the Warsaw Philharmonic was a success. Dorota is, of course, a violinist with the Philharmonic.

20. Interview by Claude-Marie Trémois, *Télérama* (January 13, 1988).

21. Amiel, pp. 86–7.

22. Ibid., p. 66.

23. Ibid., pp. 67–8. In August of 1998, Slawomir Idziak told me that he was the one who created the filters which he used (for the first time) in *A Short Film about Killing*. After Kieslowski showed him the screenplay, Idziak told him, "I can't even read this! It disgusts me," and finally conceded, "I'll shoot it only on the condition that you let me do it green and use all my filters, with which I'll darken the image." Kieslowski was not pleased, but he accepted the ultimatum—telling Idziak, "If you want to make green shit, it's your affair." The cinematographer concluded, "That's how the graphic concept came about for the film about which *Cahiers du cinéma* wrote that it was the most originally shot movie in the Cannes Film Festival."

24. When Kieslowski proposed to the Minister of Culture the expanded theatrical version of *Decalogue, 5*—at half the cost of a feature—he promised a second film for the same price and let him choose which one. *Decalogue, 6* was the Ministry's selection, resulting in *A Short Film about Love* (Amiel, pp. 96–7). But at a press conference in Boston in January 1995, Kieslowski said that he made the TV versions of *Decalogue, 5 and 6* after the long versions.

25. Amiel, p. 165.

26. Ibid., p. 103.

27. At a New York Film Festival press conference, Kieslowski enjoyed recounting that he has received numerous queries about

Van Den Budenmayer from around the world. Some have refused to believe that it is a pseudonym for Preisner, and a Dutch encyclopedia even has an entry on Van Den Budenmayer (including date of birth and death). Others have warned that Preisner will be sued if he continues to plagiarize the Dutch composer!

28. Insdorf, *The New York Times*. In an unpublished manuscript of 1997, Columbia University student Rahul Hamid explores the absence of a simple one-to-one correspondence between each *Decalogue* episode and a commandment. His chart, reprinted here, is a useful guide.

Each episode relates to one, several, or no main Commandments and secondary Commandments. The main Commandments are the major theme and the secondary Commandments are raised in some significant way during the episode.

The Episodes of *Decalogue* and their corresponding Commandments.

EPISODE	MAIN COMMANDMENT(S)	SECONDARY COMMANDMENT(S)
Decalogue, 1	Thou shalt have no other gods before me.	Honor thy father and thy mother. Thou shalt not make unto thee any graven image.
Decalogue, 2	Thou shalt have no other gods before me.	Thou shalt not kill. Thou shalt not commit adultery. Thou shalt not bear false witness against thy neighbor.
Decalogue, 3	Remember the Sabbath day, to keep it holy.	Thou shalt not bear false witness against thy neighbor. Thou shalt not kill. Thou shalt not commit adultery.
Decalogue, 4	Honor thy father and thy mother.	Thou shalt not bear false witness against thy neighbor. Thou shalt not commit adultery.
Decalogue, 5	Thou shalt not kill.	
Decalogue, 6	NONE	Thou shalt not steal. Thou shalt not bear false witness against thy neighbor. Thou shalt not kill.

EPISODE	MAIN COMMANDMENT(S)	SECONDARY COMMANDMENT
Decalogue, 7	Thou shalt not steal.	Honor thy father and thy mother. Thou shalt not bear false witness against thy neighbor.
Decalogue, 8	Thou shalt not take the name of the Lord thy God in vain. Thou shalt not bear false witness against thy neighbor.	Thou shalt not kill.
Decalogue, 9	Thou shalt not commit adultery.	Thou shalt not bear false witness against thy neighbor. Thou shalt not kill.
Decalogue, 10	Thou shalt not covet thy neighbor's house, thou shalt not covet thy neighbor's wife, nor his manservant, nor his maidservant, nor his ox, nor his ass, nor any thing that is thy neighbor's.	Thou shalt not commit adultery. Thou shalt not kill. Remember the Sabbath day, to keep it holy. Thou shalt not steal. Thou shalt have no other gods before me. Thou shalt not bear false witness against thy neighbor. Honor thy father and thy mother. Thou shalt not make unto thee any graven image.

CHAPTER 5. *THE DOUBLE LIFE OF VERONIQUE*

1. Interview with Michel Ciment and Hubert Niogret, *Positif* (June 1991), no. 364, reprinted in Amiel, pp. 114–15.

2. Ibid., pp. 115–16.

3. Kieslowski chooses the most politically charged European year, 1968, but veers immediately from the political to the personal. Similarly, he places the brief encounter between Veronique and Veronika in the context of a Kraków demonstration: while hun-

dreds are protesting in the square, our attention is drawn exclusively to the mystery of two women's identities

4. Slawomir Idziak's warm yellow filter is the opposite of the cold green filter he used in *A Short Film about Killing* (*Kieslowski on Kieslowski*, p. 186).

5. As the director put it, "When your heart stops, the line on the ECK goes straight." (Ibid., p. 185.)

6. The exploitative quality of the director's craft can also be seen in his confession to Leonardo de la Fuente: "One day, he floored me," the producer revealed. "Although he rarely uses cinematic references, he suddenly said to me, 'I made Veronika die 27 minutes into the film—like Janet Leigh in *Psycho*.'" From an Interview with Pierre Murat, *Télérama* (September 1993), p. 81.

7. Harvey Weinstein, "In Memoriam—Krzysztof Kieslowski: To Smoke and Drink in L.A.," *Premiere* (June 1996).

8. Interview with Claude-Marie Trémois and Vincent Remy, *Télérama* (September 1993), p. 91. All subsequent *Télérama* references are to this issue.

9. Amiel, p. 116.

CHAPTER 6. *THREE COLORS: BLUE*

1. *Télérama* (September 1993), p. 72. Kryzsyztof Piesiewicz interviewed by Claude-Marie Trémois.

2. Although Kieslowski denied that he was alluding to *Hiroshima, Mon Amour* by casting Emmanuelle Riva, the shot of Julie scraping her knuckles alongside the brick wall of her home recalls how Riva scrapes her knuckles on the cellar wall of Resnais's film.

3. Interview with Michel Ciment and Hubert Niogret, *Positif* (September 1993), no. 391, reprinted in Amiel, p. 130.

4. Jean-Claude Laureux interviewed by Vincent Remy, *Télérama* (September 1993), p. 78.

5. Back in his student days at the Lodz Film School, cinematographer Slawomir Idziak had already experimented with the image of

sexual embrace against a window. In Grzegorz Krolikiewicz's *Everyone Gets What He Doesn't Need* (1966), the faces of a man and woman are pressed against glass, underwater, during lovemaking.

6. It is not clear whether the eye is Olivier's and the naked back Julie's, or vice versa. But since the camera pans from the reflecting eye to Julie, we are probably seeing Olivier's eye containing her.

7. When asked if Julie composed her husband's music, Kieslowski said, "I myself am not certain what her role was. For Marin Karmitz, she wrote the music; for me, no. . . . If she sees a score, she is capable of correcting it." In Amiel, pp. 127–8.

8. Kieslowski acknowledged that the baby's image on the sonogram, absent from the script, was suggested by his assistant during production. In Amiel, p. 129.

9. What has not been taken away, Julie discards. Seated before the fire in her now-empty home, she throws away her address book after dialing Olivier's number. Although the camera does not show the book—or the other contents of her bag—in the fire, the sound of her tossing is accompanied by the flaring of the flames.

10. *Télérama,* pp. 69 and 73.

11. Krzysztof Kieslowski and Krzysztof Piesiewicz, *Three Colours Trilogy: Blue, White, Red,* translated by Danusia Stok (London: Faber and Faber, 1998), pp. 18–20. All subsequent screenplay references are to this edition.

CHAPTER 7. *THREE COLORS: WHITE*

1. Interview by Steven Gaydos, *Variety,* March 21–7, 1994, p. 55.

2. Stuart Klawans, *The Nation* (December 12, 1994), p. 739.

3. Zbigniew Zamachowski's credits include playing Mozart in the Polish production of *Amadeus.*

4. *Télérama,* p. 96.

5. Ibid., p. 93.

6. Ibid., p. 96.

7. Amiel, p. 172.

8. Paul Coates, "The Sense of an Ending," *Film Quarterly* (Winter 1996–7), vol. 50, no. 2, p. 24.

CHAPTER 8. *THREE COLORS: RED*

1. The fluid omniscience of the camera in *Red* is partly a result of the Technocrane, an expensive instrument that Kieslowski requested for the first scene connecting Valentine with Auguste and for the imaginary "fall" of the Judge's book. According to Pierre Murat, who chronicled the shooting of *Red,* "This is the first time that we are seeing [the Technocrane] in France. For the moment, only Spielberg uses this costly toy fluently." (*Télérama,* p. 48).

2. *In Camera* (Autumn 1994), p. 4.

3. Janet Maslin, *The New York Times,* October 4, 1994.

4. My (unpublished) interview with Kieslowski at the Cannes Film Festival, May 17, 1994.

5. Klawans, *The Nation,* p. 739. The theme of impotence is invoked by the music, since Kieslowski uses that of *Decalogue, 9*—where Roman's impotence makes him suicidal—when the Judge writes his letters of self-denunciation.

6. My interview at the 1994 Cannes Film Festival. During this conversation, Kieslowski specifically alluded to Kierkegaard's short novel, *Repetition*: "Maybe you can repeat something, but better. We all have made mistakes."

7. The seventh survivor of the ferry accident is English bartender Steven Killian, conspicuous in his photographic absence. To the question of who Killian might be, Kieslowski answered enigmatically, "Someone about whom a film should be made."

8. Valentine's mother is part of the sexual betrayal theme: as Valentine confesses to the Judge, her brother learned at the age of fifteen that he was not his father's son.

9. Kieslowski termed *Red* "a story of isolation," and therefore chose Switzerland, "an island in the middle of Europe." (*Télérama,* p. 96).

10. Anthony Lane, *The New Yorker* (November 28, 1994), p. 156.

11. Amiel, p. 147.

12. Dave Kehr, "To Save the World: Kieslowski's *Three Colors* Trilogy," *Film Comment* (November–December, 1994) pp. 18–20.

13. Klawans, *The Nation*, p. 738.

14. Amiel, p. 146.

15. Ibid., p. 160.

16. *Télérama*, p. 73.

17. *Kehr, Film Comment*, pp. 13, 18.

18. *Etudes Universitaires*, pp. 161–2.

EPILOGUE

1. *Kieslowski on Kieslowski*, p. 63.

2. Amiel, p. 173.

3. Harvey Weinstein, *Premiere*.

MUCH OF the following material is based on lists compiled by Danusia Stok for *Kieslowski on Kieslowski*.

For those films available on videocassette, the information appears under the credits. For Facets Multimedia (Chicago), call 1-800-331-6197. For Home Film Festival (Pennsylvania), call 1-800-258-3456.

All screenplays are by Kieslowski unless otherwise indicated.

WFD refers to Wytwornia Filmow Dokumentalnych, the State Documentary Film Studio.

The Tram (Tramwaj), 1966
Fiction short: 6 mins.
Cinematography: Zdzislaw Kaczmarek
Production: Lodz Film School (Artistic Supervisor: Wanda
    Jakubowska)
Cast: Jerzy Braszka, Maria Janiec

The Office (Urzad), 1966
Documentary short: 6 mins.
Cinematography: Lechoslaw Trzesowski
Production: Lodz Film School

Concert of Requests (Koncert Zyczen), 1967
Fiction short: 17 mins.
Cinematography: Lechoslaw Trzesowski
Production: Lodz Film School (Artistic Supervisor: Wanda
    Jakubowska)

The Photograph (Zdjecie), 1968
Documentary short: 32 mins.
Cinematography: Marek Jozwiak
Production: Polish Television

From the City of Lodz (Z Miasta Lodzi), 1969
Documentary short: 17 mins.
Cinematography: Janusz Kreczmanski, Piotr Kwiatkowski, Stanislaw Niedbalski
Production: WFD

I Was A Soldier (Bylem Zolnierzem), 1970
Documentary short: 16 mins.
Screenplay: Kieslowski and Ryszard Zgorecki
Cinematography: Stanislaw Niedbalski
Production: Czolowka

Factory (Fabryka), 1970
Documentary short: 17 mins.
Cinematography: Stanislaw Niedbalski, Jacek Tworek
Production: WFD

Before the Rally (Przed Rajdem), 1971
Documentary short: 15 mins.
Cinematography: Piotr Kwiatkowski, Jacek Petrycki
Production: WFD

Refrain (Refren), 1972
Documentary short: 10 mins.
Cinematography: Witold Stok
Production: WFD

Between Wroclaw and Zielona Gora (Miedzy Wroclawiem a Zielona Gora), 1972
Documentary short: 10 mins.
Cinematography: Jacek Petrycki
Production: WFD, commissioned by the Lubin Copper Mine

The Principles of Safety and Hygiene in a Copper Mine (Podstawy BHP W Kopalni Miedzi), 1972
Documentary short: 21 mins.
Cinematography: Jacek Petrycki
Production: WFD, commissioned by the Lubin Copper Mine

Workers '71: Nothing About Us Without Us (Robotnicy '71: Nic O Nas Bez Nas), 1972
Documentary short: 46 mins.

Directors: Kieslowski, Tomasz Zygadlo, Wojciech Wiszniewski,
    Pawel Kedzierski, Tadeusz Walendowski
Cinematography: Witold Stok, Stanislaw Mroziuk, Jacek Petrycki
Production: WFD

Bricklayer (Murarz), 1973
Documentary short: 17 mins.
Cinematography: Witold Stok
Production: WFD

Pedestrian Subway (Przejscie Podziemne), 1973
Fiction short: 30 mins.
Screenplay: Ireneusz Iredynski and Kieslowski
Cinematography: Slawomir Idziak
Production: Polish Television
Cast: Teresa Budzisz-Krzyzanowska, Andrzej Seweryn

X-Ray (Przeswietlenie), 1974
Documentary short: 13 mins.
Cinematography: Jacek Petrycki
Production: WFD

First Love (Pierwsza Milosc), 1974
Documentary short: 30 mins.
Cinematography: Jacek Petrycki
Production: Polish Television

Curriculum Vitae (Zyciorys), 1975
Documentary/fiction short: 45 mins.
Screenplay: Janusz Fastyn and Kieslowski
Cinematography: Jacek Petrycki, Tadeusz Rusinek
Production: WFD

Personnel (Personel), 1975
Fiction featurette: 72 mins.
Cinematography: Witold Stok
Production: Polish Television
Cast: Juliusz Machulski (Romek), Michal Tarkowski (Sowa)

Hospital (Szpital), 1976
Documentary short: 21 mins.
Cinematography: Jacek Petrycki
Production: WFD

The Scar (Blizna), 1976
Fiction feature: 104 mins.
Screenplay: Romuald Karas and Kieslowski, based on a story by
  Karas
Cinematography: Slawomir Idziak
Production: Tor
Cast: Franciszek Pieczka (Stefan Bednarz), Jerzy Stuhr, Mariusz
  Dmochowski

Slate (Klaps), 1976
Out-takes from *The Scar:* 6 mins.

The Calm (Spokoj), 1976
Fiction featurette: 70 mins.
Screenplay: Kieslowski and Jerzy Stuhr, based on a story by Lech
  Borski
Cinematography: Jacek Petrycki
Production: Polish Television
Cast: Jerzy Stuhr (Antek Gralak), Izabella Olszewska, Jerzy Trela

*From A Night Porter's Point of View (Z Punktu Widzenia Nocnego
  Portiera),* 1977
Documentary short: 17 mins.
Cinematography: Witold Stok
Music: Wojciech Kilar
Production: WFD

I Don't Know (Nie Wiem), 1977
Documentary short: 46 mins.
Cinematography: Jacek Petrycki
Production: WFD

Seven Women of Different Ages (Siedem Kobiet W Roznym Wieku), 1978
Documentary short: 16 mins.
Cinematography: Witold Stok
Production: WFD

Camera Buff (Amator), 1979
Fiction feature: 112 mins.
Screenplay: Kieslowski and Jerzy Stuhr
Cinematography: Jacek Petrycki

Production: Tor
Cast: Jerzy Stuhr (Filip Mosz), Malgorzata Zabkowska (Irka), Ewa
  Pokas (Anna), Stefan Czyzewski (Manager), Jerzy Nowak (Osuch),
  Tadeusz Bradecki (Witek), Krzysztof Zanussi (himself)
Available on video, including Facets and Home Film Festival.

Station (Dworzec), 1980
Documentary short: 13 mins.
Cinematography: Witold Stok
Production: WFD

Talking Heads (Gadajace Glowy), 1980
Documentary short: 16 mins.
Cinematography: Jacek Petrycki, Piotr Kwiatkowski
Production: WFD

Blind Chance (Przypadek), 1981
Fiction feature: 122 mins.
Cinematography: Krzysztof Pakulski
Music: Wojciech Kilar
Production: Tor
Cast: Boguslaw Linda (Witek), Tadeusz Lomnicki (Werner), Bogus-
  lawa Pawelec (Czuszka), Monika Gozdzik (Olga)
Available on video, including Facets and Home Film Festival.

A Short Working Day (Krotki Dzien Pracy), 1981
Fiction feature: 79 mins.
Screenplay: Kieslowski and Hanna Krall, based on Krall's *View from a
  First Floor Window*
Cinematography: Krzysztof Pakulski
Production: Polish Television

No End (Bez Konca), 1984
Fiction feature: 107 mins.
Screenplay: Kieslowski and Krzysztof Piesiewicz
Cinematography: Jacek Petrycki
Music: Zbigniew Preisner
Production: Tor
Cast: Grazyna Szapolowska (Urszula), Jerzy Radziwillowicz (Antoni),
  Maria Pakulnis (Joanna), Aleksander Bardini (Labrador), Artur
  Barcis (Dariusz)
Available on video, including Facets and Home Film Festival.

Seven Days a Week (Siedem Dni W Tygodniu), 1988
Documentary short: 18 mins.
Cinematography: Jacek Petrycki
Production: City Life, Rotterdam

A Short Film about Killing (Krotki Film O Zabijaniu), 1988
Fiction feature: 85 mins.
Screenplay: Kieslowski and Krzysztof Piesiewicz
Cinematography: Slamowir Idziak
Music: Zbigniew Preisner
Production: Tor and Polish Television
Cast: Miroslaw Baka (Jacek), Jan Tesarz (Taxi-driver), Krzysztof Globisz (Piotr)

A Short Film about Love (Krotki Film O Milosci), 1988
Fiction feature: 87 mins.
Screenplay: Kieslowski and Krzysztof Piesiewicz
Cinematography: Witold Adamek
Music: Zbigniew Preisner
Production: Tor and Polish Television
Cast: Grazyna Szapolowska (Magda), Olaf Lubaszenko (Tomek), Stefania Iwinska (Landlady)

The Decalogue (Dekalog), 1988
Ten fiction featurettes of approximately 55 minutes each.
Screenplay: Kieslowski and Krzysztof Piesiewicz
Music: Zbigniew Preisner
Editor: Ewa Smal
Art Director: Halina Dobrowolska
Producer: Ryszard Chutkowski
Production: Polish Television
Cast: Artur Barcis (The Young Man)
Available in certain video stores, and on PAL from Facets.

Decalogue, 1: 53 mins. Cinematography: Wieslaw Zdort
Cast: Henryk Baranowski (Krzysztof), Wojciech Klata (Pawel), Maja Komorowska (Irena)

Decalogue, 2: 57 mins. Cinematography: Edward Klosinski.
Cast: Krystyna Janda (Dorota), Aleksander Bardini (Doctor), Olgerd Lukaszewicz (Andrzej)

Decalogue, 3: 56 mins. Cinematography: Piotr Sobocinski
Cast: Daniel Olbrychski (Janusz), Maria Pakulnis (Eva)

Decalogue, 4: 55 mins. Cinematography: Krzysztof Pakulski
Cast: Adrianna Biedrzynska (Anka), Janusz Gajos (Michal)

Decalogue, 5: 57 mins. Cinematography: Slawomir Idziak
Cast: Miroslaw Baka (Jacek), Krzysztof Globisz (Piotr), Jan Tesarz
(Taxi-driver), Zbigniew Zapasiewicz (Law school examiner)

Decalogue, 6: 58 mins. Cinematography: Witold Adamek
Cast: Grazyna Szaplowska (Magda), Olaf Lubaszenko (Tomek), Stefania Iwinska (Landlady)

Decalogue, 7: 55 mins. Cinematography: Dariusz Kuc
Cast: Anna Polony (Eva), Maja Barelkowska (Majka), Wladyslaw
Kowalski (Stefan), Boguslaw Linda (Wojtek)

Decalogue, 8: 55 mins. Cinematography: Andrzej Jaroszewicz
Cast: Maria Koscialkowska (Zofia), Teresa Marczewska (Elzbieta),
Tadeusz Lomnicki (Tailor)

Decalogue, 9: 58 mins. Cinematography: Piotr Sobocinski
Cast: Ewa Blaszczyk (Hanka), Piotr Machalica (Roman), Jan
Jankowski (Mariusz), Jolanta Pietek-Gorecka (Ola)

Decalogue, 10: 57 mins. Cinematography: Jacek Blawut
Cast: Jerzy Stuhr (Jerzy), Zbigniew Zamachowski (Artur), Henryk
Bista (Shopkeeper)

The Double Life of Veronique (La Double Vie de Veronique), 1991
Fiction feature: 96 mins.
Screenplay: Kieslowski and Krzysztof Piesiewicz
Cinematography: Slawomir Idziak
Music: Zbigniew Preisner
Editor: Jacques Witta
Producer: Leonardo de la Fuente
Production: Sideral Productions/Tor/Le Studio Canal Plus
Cast: Irene Jacob (Veronika/Veronique), Philippe Volter (Alexan-
dre), Wladyslaw Kowalski (Veronika's father), Claude Duneton
(Veronique's father)
Available on videocassette.

Three Colors: Blue (Bleu), 1993
Fiction feature: 98 mins.
Screenplay: Kieslowski and Krzysztof Piesiewicz
Cinematography: Slawomir Idziak
Music: Zbigniew Preisner
Editor: Jacques Witta
Producer: Marin Karmitz
Production: MK2/Tor/et al.
Cast: Juliette Binoche (Julie), Benoit Régent (Olivier), Florence Per-
nel (Sandrine), Charlotte Very (Lucille), Emmanuelle Riva (Julie's
mother)
Available on videocassette.

Three Colors: White (Blanc), 1993
Fiction feature: 90 mins.
Screenplay: Kieslowski and Krzysztof Piesiewicz
Cinematography: Edward Klosinski
Music: Zbigniew Preisner
Editor: Urszula Lesiak
Producer: Marin Karmitz
Production: Tor/MK2/et al.
Cast: Zbigniew Zamachowski (Karol), Julie Delpy (Dominique),
Janusz Gajos (Mikolay), Jerzy Stuhr (Jurek)
Available on videocassette.

Three Colors: Red (Rouge), 1994
Fiction feature: 95 mins.
Screenplay: Kieslowski and Krzysztof Piesiewicz
Cinematography: Piotr Sobocinski
Music: Zbigniew Preisner
Editor: Jacques Witta
Producer: Marin Karmitz
Production: CAB productions/MK2/Tor/ et al.
Cast: Irene Jacob (Valentine), Jean-Louis Trintignant (The Judge),
Jean-Pierre Lorit (Auguste), Frédérique Feder (Karin)
Available on videocassette.

Camouflage (Barwy Ochronne), 1977, Poland
Director: Krzysztof Zanussi
In Polish with English subtitles.
Available on video.

Confidentially Yours (Vivement Dimanche!), 1983, France
Director: François Truffaut
In French with English subtitles.
Available on video.

Krzysztof Kieslowski: I'm So-So, 1995, Denmark/Poland
Documentary: 56 mins.
Director: Krzysztof Wierzbicki
Made for Television, in Polish with English subtitles.
Available on video, including Home Film Festival.

The Last Stage (Ostatni Etap), 1948, Poland
Director: Wanda Jakubowska
In Polish with English subtitles.
Available on video, including Facets.

The Noose (Petla), 1957, Poland
Director: Wojciech Has

An Uneventful Story (Nieciekawa Historia), 1982, Poland
Director: Wojciech Has

Wings of Desire, 1988, Germany/France
Director: Wim Wenders
In German with English subtitles.
Available on videocassette.

BOOKS CITED:

Amiel, Vincent (ed.). *Krzysztof Kieslowski: Textes réunis et présentés par Vincent Amiel*. Paris: POSITIF/Jean-Michel Place, 1997. Includes essays and interviews by Michel Ciment, Jacques Demeure, Jean Gili, Hubert Niogret.

Campan, Véronique. *Dix brèves histoires d'image: Le Décalogue de Krzysztof Kieslowski*. Paris: Presses de la Sorbonne Nouvelle, 1993.

Davies, Norman. *Heart of Europe: A Short History of Poland*. New York: Oxford University Press, 1986.

Estève, Michel (ed.). *Etudes Cinématographiques: Krzysztof Kieslowski*. Paris: Lettres Modernes, 1994. Includes essays by Joel Magny, Agnes Peck, René Prédal.

Kieslowski, Krzysztof and Krzysztof Piesiewicz. *Decalogue: The Ten Commandments*. Trans. Phil Cavendish and Susannah Bluh. London and Boston: Faber and Faber, 1991.

Kieslowski, Krzysztof and Krzysztof Piesiewicz. *Three Colors Trilogy: Blue, White, Red*. Trans. Danusia Stok. London: Faber and Faber, 1998.

Stok, Danusia (ed. and trans.). *Kieslowski on Kieslowski*. London and Boston: Faber and Faber, 1993.

Télérama (hors-série/special issue). *La Passion Kieslowski*. Paris: September 1993. Includes interviews by Pierre Murat, Vincent Remy, Claude-Marie Trémois.

ADDITIONAL BOOKS:

Bren, Frank. *World Cinema I: Poland*. London: Flicks Books, 1986.

Fuksiewicz, Jacek. *Le Cinéma Polonais*. Paris: Les Editions du Cerf, 1989.

Garbowski, Christopher. *Krzysztof Kieslowski's Decalogue Series: The Problem of the Protagonists and Their Self-Transcendance*. (sic) Boulder:

East European Monographs, 1996. (Distributed by Columbia University Press.)

Kuszewski, Stanislaw. *Contemporary Polish Film.* Warsaw: Interpress Publishers, 1978.

Paul, David (ed.). *Politics, Art and Commitment in Eastern European Cinema.* London: Macmillan Press, 1983.

Zawislinski, Stanislaw (ed.). *Kieslowski.* Warsaw: Wydawnictwo Skorpion, 1996. Photo album plus Kieslowski's journal entries. ISBN 83-86466-11-1.

Zawislinski, Stanislaw (ed.). *Kieslowski, Znany i Nieznany.* Warsaw: PWP Sprint, 1998. Publication based on the symposium, "Kieslowski, Known and Unknown," organized in Warsaw, March 12-13, 1998. ISBN 83-864-66-17-0.

Zawislinski, Stanislaw (ed.). *O Kieslowskim.* Warsaw: Wydawnictwo Skorpion, 1998. Includes reminiscences by Agnieszka Holland, Marin Karmitz, Krzysztof Piesiewicz, Zbigniew Preisner, Jerzy Stuhr, Andrzej Wajda, and Krzysztof Zanussi. ISBN 83-86466-18-9.

SELECTED ARTICLES:

Coates, Paul. "The Sense of an Ending," *Film Quarterly* 50, 2, Winter 1996-97.

Corliss, Richard. "The Best of 1998," *Time Magazine,* December 21, 1998.

Dupont, Joan. "Film Variations in Red, White and Blue," *International Herald Tribune,* August 31, 1993.

Gaydos, Steven. "Pole Vaults Past Biz Blocks," *Variety,* March 21–27, 1994.

In Camera (no author listed), "Coloring the Message," Autumn 1994.

Insdorf, Annette. "Born in the Ruins of War, a School Flowered," *The New York Times* (Arts and Leisure), December 13, 1998.

Insdorf, Annette. "*The Decalogue* Re-examines God's Commands," *The New York Times* (Arts and Leisure), October 28, 1990.

Insdorf, Annette. "Director Commands Respect," *Chicago Sun-Times,* Sunday, October 15, 1989.

Kehr, Dave. "To Save the World: Kieslowski's *Three Colors* Trilogy," *Film Comment,* November–December 1994.

Klawans, Stuart. Review of *Three Colors: Red, The Nation,* December 12, 1994.

Kornatowska, Maria. " ' . . . Yet We Do Not Know What Will Become of Us': On the Artistic Output of Wojciech Jerzy Has," *Bulletin de la Société des Sciences et des Lettres de Lodz* VI, 1995.

Lane, Anthony. "Red Blues," *The New Yorker*, November 28, 1994.

Lane, Anthony. "Starting Over," *The New Yorker*, December 13, 1993.

Maslin, Janet. Review of *Three Colors: Red, The New York Times*, October 4, 1994.

Peña, Richard. Catalogue notes for The Walter Reade Theater, New York, September–October 1997.

Sherman, Betsy. "Kieslowski Uncovers Poetic Mystery in the Everyday," *The Boston Sunday Globe*, January 23, 1994.

Siegel, Joshua. Catalogue essay for "The Lodz Film School of Poland: 50 Years," Museum of Modern Art, New York, December 1998.

Weinstein, Harvey. "In Memoriam—Krzysztof Kieslowski: To Smoke and Drink in L.A.," *Premiere*, June 1996.

TAPED MATERIAL CITED:

Boston: *Red* press conference, sponsored by the French Library and Cultural Center, January 25, 1995.

New York: *Blue* press conference, New York Film Festival, October 5, 1993, videotaped by Tom Farrell.

New York: *Red* press conference, New York Film Festival, October 3, 1994, videotaped by Tom Farrell.

Paris: Colloquium devoted to Kieslowski's work at the Paris Vidéothèque, June 17, 1997 (audiotape from MK2).

Paris: *Kieslowski par Kieslowski,* dir. Dominique Rabourdin, La Sept, 1994. TV documentary.

Paris: *La Leçon du Cinéma,* dir. Dominique Rabourdin and Andrzej Wolski, La Sept-Arte, 1994. TV documentary.

Page 2: Photos by Phil Borgeson

Page 4: Collection of Annette Insdorf

Page 12: Courtesy of Stanislaw Zawislinski

Pages 16, 18–20, 22, 25–28, 34: Courtesy of Warsaw Documentary Film Studio

Pages 29, 32: Copyright Rotterdam Films, photos by Dirk Rijneke

Pages 39, 42, 44, 55, 59, 61, 62, 65, 67: Courtesy of Film Polski

Pages 72, 77, 82, 85, 87, 105, 115, 116, 122: Courtesy of Poltel

Pages 80, 89, 90, 93, 100, 104: Courtesy of Museum of Modern Art/Film Stills Archive

Pages 108, 110: Photos by Andrzej Burchard

Pages 126, 129: Courtesy of Miramax Films, photos by Monika Jeziorowska

Page 136: Courtesy of Leonardo de la Fuente

Pages 132, 134, 145, 147, 149, 161, 168, 176, 180: Frame enlargements from 35mm prints courtesy of Miramax Films

INDEX

ANNETTE INSDORF is a Professor in the Graduate Film Division of Columbia University's School of the Arts, as well as Director of Undergraduate Film Studies. From 1990 to 1995, she was Chair of the Film Division. She taught film history and criticism at Yale University from 1975 till 1988.

Dr. Insdorf is the author of *François Truffaut,* a study of the French director's work: the updated edition was reissued in 1995 by Cambridge University Press. After the first publication of the book in 1978, she also served as his translator. Considered an authority on the French New Wave, she provided the voice-over commentary for the laser-disc package of Truffaut's films released by the Criterion collection and was one of the people interviewed in the French documentary *François Truffaut: Stolen Portaits* (1993).

Her second book, *Indelible Shadows: Film and the Holocaust,* is considered a landmark study in the subject. The revised edtion, with a preface by Elie Wiesel, was published in 1990. Among the places where she has lectured on this topic are the U.S. Holocaust Museum, the Smithsonian Institution, and Princeton University.

Dr. Insdorf was born in Paris and moved to New York where she received her B.A. from Queens College and her Ph.D. from Yale University, as a Danforth Fellow. In 1986, she was named *Chevalier dans l'ordre des arts et des lettres* by the French Ministry of Culture. A second honor followed in 1993, when she was "knighted" *dans l'ordre des palmes académiques.*

She has been a frequent contributor to *The New York Times* Arts and Leisure section, and her articles have appeared in *The San Francisco Chronicle, Premiere, The Los Angeles Times, Film Comment, The Washington Post,* and *Rolling Stone.*

On television, Dr. Insdorf co-hosts (with Roger Ebert) Cannes Film Festival coverage for BRAVO/IFC; has served as host for

TéléFrance Ciné-Club (a national cable-TV program); for *Years of Darkness* (an eight-week series of films about the World War II experience shown by WNET/PBS); and for WNYC-TV. Guest appearances include *The Charlie Rose Show*, CINEMAX, A & E, CUNY-TV, and numerous interviews on French and British TV.

She was a jury member at the 1998 Berlin Film Festival. A popular panel moderator, she is responsible for all the panels at the annual Telluride Film Festival (where she is also the main translator) and often performs this role for the Independent Feature Project, Women in Film, Miami Film Festival, and the Cannes Film Festival. Since 1983, she has been offering an annual film series at New York's 92nd Street Y; her guests have included Martin Scorsese, Jeremy Irons, Pedro Almodovar, Susan Sarandon, David Puttnam, Oliver Stone, and Al Pacino.

Dr. Insdorf is the executive producer of *Shoeshine*, nominated for an Academy Award for the Best Live-Action Short of 1987. The 10-minute movie starring Jerry Stiller and Ben Stiller also won the Grand Prize at the Montreal Film Festival. In addition, she served as executive producer of *Short-Term Bonds*—a 9-minute film that won a CINE Golden Eagle—and *Performance Pieces,* starring F. Murray Abraham, named Best Fiction Short at the 1989 Cannes Film Festival.